Thinking Through Job

L. A. Mott, Jr.

DeWard
PUBLISHING COMPANY

Thinking Through Job
© 2011 by DeWard Publishing Company, Ltd.
P.O. Box 6259, Chillicothe, Ohio 45601
800.300.9778
www.dewardpublishing.com

Unless otherwise noted, all Scripture quotations are from the American Standard Version of the Bible. Italics from the ASV text have been retained, and ASV footnotes have been inserted into the text in brackets. Any emphasis to the Biblical text has been added by the author.

Reasonable care has been taken to trace original sources for any excerpts and quotations appearing in this book and to document such information. For material not in the public domain, fair-use standards and practices were followed. Should any attribution be found to be incorrect or incomplete, the publisher welcomes written documentation supporting correction for subsequent printings.

Printed in the United States of America.

ISBN: 978-1-936341-06-1

In Loving Memory of Homer Hailey

…with whom I studied with unmixed pleasure for three years in the '50s, who taught me to love the scriptures at a higher level, and whom I will always consider a special gift of God to me. The Lord supplied the church with apostles, prophets, evangelists, pastors and teachers (Eph 4.11). He gave me and many others Homer Hailey.

I had formed most of my views on Job by the time Brother Hailey was completing his book on Job, and he asked me, as well as others, to read his manuscript. He said he wanted it to be his best work. I took him at his word and did my best to help. I wrote notes all through his manuscript and on many, many yellow pages. I was especially anxious to change his view on the role of Elihu. But it was too late, and I do not think I had any major effect. I was probably expecting too much of someone who thought his work was already done for the most part. I wrote too much and perhaps too frankly, and about all I succeeded in doing was to upset him a little as I learned from a mutual friend. At age 72 I am beginning to understand how he might have felt.

But he returned the manuscript at my request with all my scribbling in black and his own numerous responses in red. It may be my greatest treasure, and the notes in red are a model of a gracious and humble spirit in one who had attained such an advanced age.

Nothing that I have written here should be understood as expressing the least disrespect toward this man whose greatness puts me altogether in the shade by comparison. (He should have listened to me on Elihu, however.)

CONTENTS

ABBREVIATIONS

AB	Anchor Bible
ASV	American Standard Version (1901)
BDB	The New Brown – Driver – Briggs – Gesenius Hebrew and English Lexicon
Ges.	Gesenius Hebrew-Chaldee Lexicon of the Old Testament
ICC	International Critical Commentary
KJV	King James Version
NASB	New American Standard Bible
NEB	New English Bible
NIV	New International Version
NKJV	New King James Version
RSV	Revised Standard Version

Principal Commentaries Consulted for *Thinking Through Job*

S R. Driver in ICC   William H. Green
A B. Davidson   Homer Hailey
Francis I. Anderson   G. Raulerson, Pulpit Commentarry
Franz Delitzsch   H. H. Rowley

...the ones I recall. I have not read everything. I am not that kind of scholar. I read till I think I see what can be said on a passage and then formulate my own view. The reader will also perceive that I used several standard translations. I try to refrain from merely regurgitating the positions of earlier writers, and to do my own study and thinking. The more thorough students of Job will have to judge the extent to which I succeeded.

PREFACE

The Bible contains testimony and evidence to create faith. My *Thinking Through John* deals with one of the books that is expressly written for that purpose (*cf.* John 20.30f). But the Bible also contains material to support and strengthen faith when it is under trial; material to answer the problems of faith. The Book of Job is among the portions of scripture that speak to these ends.

I cannot claim, as Homer Hailey could, that I have suffered physically as Job did. But Job's physical afflictions were not the primary (or greatest) trial to his faith. The greater trial lay in what these afflictions seem to imply with regard to his relationship with God, and the way he appeared to be shut off from communion with God. I well understand such psychological trial. And perhaps many others will as well. If you have ever felt cut off from God, if communications with God seem to have broken down, then the Book of Job may speak to your heart and possibly be the medicine that ministers to and saves your faith.

Have you ever considered the world and its perplexities and wondered why things are the way they are? Why does God permit the evils? Why is this happening to me? Why is there injustice in the world?

Have you ever felt that you were living in the darkness? Have you ever wished for some explanation, but felt that God has left you in the dark? Have you felt isolated and alone, alienated from God, or even that God is treating you as an enemy?

If you have experienced any of these perplexities, the Book of Job can speak to you. True, the problem of human suffering, and especially the suffering of a good man, receives primary attention. But one need not suffer like Job in order to experience the problems that were so perplexing to Job. In fact, the sense of alienation from God, the impression that God was acting with hostility toward him and treating him unfairly, was Job's greatest trial rather than the physical suffering in itself. If the mysteries of divine providence have ever been a trial to your faith, then you will find in the man Job a kindred spirit. You will hear him give expression to your own trials and perplexities, and you will find in this book answers that will sustain your own faith when it is under trial.

Job has been a great blessing to me and a source to which I have turned again and again through the last half century. I hope my little book will help you to discover wondrous things in God's Word (*cf.* Psa 119.18), and that you will find in the Book of Job the rich resource that I have found it to be.

I see no way to establish the date of the book and recommend that serious students consult the scholarly commentaries for what can be said on the question. You will not be far into the study of Job before you realize that its message is one for the ages, largely unaffected by the date in which it was written. The book may have been written long after the times in which the man Job lived, and we can say a little more about these times.

The book is set in patriarchal times. The principal characters are not Israelites but live before God had a special covenant nation. Thus their arguments are sustained by appeal to "thoughts from the visions of the night" (4.12–21) and to the wisdom and experience of the ancients (8.8–10) rather than by reference to the Sinaitic covenant, though the latter contains many passages that bear on the issues discussed by Job and his friends. Job's lifespan (*cf.* 42.16) fits the patriarchal period (*cf.* Gen 25.7) more than later times (Psa 90.10). The principal name for God *the Almighty* (31 times in Job) is characteristic of the patriarchal times (Gen 17.1; 28.3; 35.11; 43.14; 48.3; 49.25; *cf.* Exod 6.3; Num 24.4, 16). Only a few occurrences date from later times. Job's approaches to God through sacrifice (1.5; 42.7–9) resemble the patriarchal times. Priests, tabernacles and/or temples are not mentioned. The unit of money (Heb. *kesitah*) referred to in 42.11 is "mentioned elsewhere only in transactions of the patriarchal age (Gen 33.19; Josh 24.32)" (Pope in AB, 291). The mention of an inheritance left by Job to his daughters (42.15) may also point to patriarchal times (compare Gen 31.14 and contrast Num 27.1–11).

But enough on this background question. I want to get you into the book as quickly as possible.

The commentary on the text is written briefly and "tightly," I would say. A reader will need to study it with the Bible open before him, for which reason I have copied the text of the American Standard Version of 1901 at the head of passages throughout the book. But sometimes the commentary is based on an even more literal rendering of the Biblical text.

Prologue

Job 1–3

A historical prologue provides background for understanding the discussion that follows. It also raises the key issues of the book, especially in the challenge put by Satan.

A Man Named Job (1.1–5)

There was a man in the land of Uz, whose name was Job [Heb. *Iyob*]; and that man was perfect and upright, and one that feared God, and turned away from evil. ²And there were born unto him seven sons and three daughters. ³His substance [Or, cattle] also was seven thousand sheep, and three thousand camels, and five hundred yoke of oxen, and five hundred she-asses, and a very great household; so that this man was the greatest of all the children of the east. ⁴And his sons went and held a feast in the house of each one upon his day; and they sent and called for their three sisters to eat and to drink with them. ⁵And it was so, when the days of their feasting were gone about, that Job sent and sanctified them, and rose up early in the morning, and offered burnt-offerings according to the number of them all: for Job said, It may be that my sons have sinned, and renounced [Or, blasphemed: see v 11; 2.5, 9] God in their hearts. Thus did Job continually.

1. Job is immediately put before us as a man of extremely good character—complete integrity, godfearing, avoiding evil (v 1). "Perfect" does not mean sinless, but complete—through and through a man of good character.

   2. He is also a man of great prosperity: large family, extensive property, in fact "the greatest (meaning the wealthiest) of all the children of the east" (vv 2–3).

   3. His offspring appear as a close knit family, regularly enjoying each other's company (v 4).

4. Job not only fears God himself but cares deeply about the spiritual wellbeing of his family (v 5).

Behind the Scenes: A Council in Heaven (1.6–12)

⁶Now it came to pass on the day when the sons of God came to present themselves before Jehovah, that Satan [That is, the Adversary] also came among them. ⁷And Jehovah said unto Satan, Whence comest thou? Then Satan answered Jehovah, and said, From going to and fro in the earth, and from walking up and down in it. ⁸And Jehovah said unto Satan, Hast thou considered my servant Job? for [Or, that] there is none like him in the earth, a perfect and an upright man, one that feareth God, and turneth away from evil. ⁹Then Satan answered Jehovah, and said, Doth Job fear God for nought? ¹⁰Hast not thou made a hedge about him, and about his house, and about all that he hath, on every side? thou hast blessed the work of his hands, and his substance [Or, cattle] is increased in the land. ¹¹But put forth thy hand now, and touch all that he hath, and he will renounce thee to thy face. ¹²And Jehovah said unto Satan, Behold, all that he hath is in thy power [Heb. *hand*]; only upon himself put not forth thy hand. So Satan went forth from the presence of Jehovah.

Occasion (6–7)

The occasion is "the day when the sons of God came to present themselves before Jehovah"—*i.e.*, as a servant stands before his superior (Prov 22.29; *cf.* 1 Sam 16.21f; Jer 52.12; Zech 6.5). (*Sons of God* is a reference to angels, as in 38.7.) It seems to be an occasion when these messengers and servants of God appear before him to report on some mission and perhaps to be assigned some new mission.

On that day "Satan (meaning adversary) also came among them" (6). Satan is the adversary of man, making charges against him, calling attention to his faults, even tempting him to do wrong (7–12; 1 Chron 21.1; Zech 3.1). Satan reports that he has been roaming about the earth (7), apparently with a view to discovering and reporting on human frailty, though his purpose is not disclosed.

Jehovah's Estimate of Job (8)

Jehovah's own estimate of Job is given in agreement with the original description (1). Job seems to be flung out as a kind of challenge to Satan. He was one man at least in whom Jehovah was confident Satan could find no fault. But observe that Job is offered not as a representative specimen, but as exceptional—"there is none like him in the earth." He is unequaled, unexampled—in short, the best man on earth. It is the best man on earth who is to be subjected to the trials that follow.

Satan's Challenge (9–11)

Satan cannot find fault with Job's life but attacks his motives. He charges that Job's piety is not genuine. His pious service is not disinterested. He only serves God for the pay. He is not really serving God but himself. If the compensation that makes Job's service so profitable to himself were taken away, then Job would renounce God to his face. Then the selfish nature of his service would be revealed, and he would be exposed as one more man who loved and served self rather than God.

So Satan appears as a cynical being who challenges whether such a thing as real piety exists in the world. It does not even exist in this man God considers the best man on earth. The experiment proposed by Satan will test the genuineness and reality of Job's piety.

But his challenge also serves to define the nature of real piety. For if man reverences God only for what he can get out of it, is he not in reality serving self rather than God? Does not real piety exist only when a person will reverence God for himself regardless of rewards and punishments?

Furthermore, Satan is not just man's adversary. He is also a bitter antagonist of Jehovah. For his challenge implies that even the best man on earth by God's own estimation will not serve God unless he is paid to do so. He takes the position that the best man on earth is not serving God solely out of faith or love for God but only out of self-interest. So the experiment will test whether God is worthy of service for his own sake. Is God so great that a person ought to worship and serve him even though it may not be profitable to himself? This book does not deal with the answer "everyman" might give to this question, but it does disclose the answer that comes from the best man on earth. We shall see what recommendation this book makes to others who must serve God in circumstances similar to Job's. What an opportunity lies before Job to give glory to God! It may be that the best opportunity any person has to give glory to God is when he suffers to the absolute limit, and still remains faithful to God. What a testimony to the greatness and the character of God!

Permission Granted (12)

Satan is not another God. He is Jehovah's inferior. He cannot act independently, but only under Jehovah's control. He cannot act without permission. That is one great thing to be learned from this scene. Satan cannot act against mankind without permission from God.

Jehovah will not himself put forth his hand against Job but grants Satan permission to perform the test and to take away Job's possessions while limiting his power against Job.

It is interesting that Satan is never mentioned in the debate over Job's suffering. Job's adversity is ascribed to God, and even at the end Job's relatives and acquaintances console him "for all the evil that Jehovah had brought on him" (42.11). I believe we give superficial explanations when we say God was not responsible, but Satan was. The concluding portions of the book, where resolution of the problem is provided, do not take this easy way out. Elihu does not. Jehovah himself does not. Satan could not act without permission. God permitted, or authorized, what Satan did. It is no error to say God was ultimately responsible. The solution to the problem discussed in this book is more complex than we make it when we try to vindicate God by putting the blame on Satan.

But what is God's motive? Satan's purpose seems pretty transparent. As the adversary of man he acts to bring him down or to disrupt his relationship with God. He is man's adversary and we expect the adversary of man to act against him. But why does Jehovah authorize and allow this cruel attack on Job? Is he also the adversary of Job, as Job will come to think (and for which opinion Job is rebuked by Elihu)? Is Jehovah also against Job rather than for him, in spite of his own testimony to the goodness of this man? Or can we somehow believe that Jehovah is on Job's side, in spite of permitting such an attack to be launched against him? What can be the divine purpose? In my opinion, it is simply impossible to believe that Jehovah permits this attack on Job for no other purpose than to silence Satan's taunt.

Job is left in the dark on these questions. Will the Book of Job leave its readers also in the dark? Or will it satisfy our minds by disclosing a divine purpose in the suffering of such a good man? Will we learn that such a trial of man's faith is really necessary in the divine scheme of things? Finally, if no divine purpose is ever disclosed, can we conclude that God is worthy of worship in any case? Is that the essence of genuine piety, *i.e.,* reverencing God regardless of reward as Satan's challenge implies?

Finally, it is important to realize that the conversation between Jehovah and Satan takes place "behind the scenes." Job is not told why he is afflicted. He must suffer without explanation. As we shall see in the course of the debate that follows, ignorance on Job's part was an important element of his pain. His greatest trial was not the physical suffering but the mental torture of thinking that God, for some undisclosed reason, had turned against him and was treating him as an enemy and as a sinner. This withholding of information from Job made for a most cruel trial, even a psychological torture. But it was essential to the test. The point could not be made without it.

The First Blow: Job Stripped of Property and Family (1.13–19)

¹³And it fell on a day when his sons and his daughters were eating and drinking wine in their eldest brother's house, ¹⁴that there came a messenger unto Job, and said, The oxen were plowing, and the asses feeding beside them; ¹⁵and the Sabeans [Heb. *Sheba*] fell *upon them*, and took them away: yea, they have slain the servants [Heb. *young men*] with the edge of the sword; and I only am escaped alone to tell thee. ¹⁶While he was yet speaking, there came also another, and said, The fire of God is fallen from heaven, and hath burned up the sheep and the servants, and consumed them; and I only am escaped alone to tell thee. ¹⁷While he was yet speaking, there came also another, and said, The Chaldeans made three bands, and fell [Or, made a raid] upon the camels, and have taken them away, yea, and slain the servants with the edge of the sword; and I only am escaped alone to tell thee. ¹⁸While he was yet speaking, there came also another, and said, Thy sons and thy daughters were eating and drinking wine in their eldest brother's house; ¹⁹and, behold, there came a great wind from [Or, over] the wilderness, and smote the four corners of the house, and it fell upon the young men, and they are dead; and I only am escaped alone to tell thee.

The accumulation of a lifetime is stripped away all in one day and Job learns about it all in a single hour. One day Job was "the greatest of all the children of the east" (3). The next day he had been stripped entirely bare. The disasters struck in four devastating blows which came without warning. Life continued on as usual (vv 13f, 18) until the disasters suddenly struck. The news comes to Job by means of four messengers:

First Messenger: The oxen and donkeys were taken away by Sabean raiders who also killed all the servants who tended them except for the messenger.

Second Messenger: "The fire of God" (extraordinary lightning?) fell from heaven and burned up the sheep and consumed the servants except for the messenger.

Third Messenger: Chaldaeans made a three-pronged raid, taking away the camels and killing the servants except for the messenger.

Fourth Messenger: A whirlwind struck the house in which Job's children were feasting, destroying the house and killing the children and their attendants except for the messenger.

So in one day "the greatest of all the children of the east" was stripped of property and family. His wife was spared, but that was no advantage since she herself soon becomes an instrument of temptation (*cf.* 2.9).

Job's Reaction (1.20–22)

²⁰Then Job arose, and rent his robe, and shaved his head, and fell down upon the ground, and worshipped; ²¹and he said, Naked came I out of my mother's womb, and naked shall I return thither: Jehovah gave, and Jehovah hath taken away; blessed be the name of Jehovah. ²²In all this Job sinned not, nor charged God foolishly [Or, attributed folly to God].

Satan had predicted that Job would renounce God to his face (11), but instead:

1. Job goes through the usual mourning rituals, and bows in homage to Jehovah (20).

2. He recognizes that his possessions are all gifts of God, who had only done at an earlier time what he would have done in any case at death. Job recognizes Jehovah's sovereign right to give and to take away and praises his name (21).

3. "In all this Job sinned not, nor attributed folly (or unworthy behavior) to God" (22, margin), as Satan suggested he surely would.

Instead of attributing some evil to Jehovah, Job has only good to say of him; only worship to offer. To this point he certainly holds that Jehovah is worthy of worship without regard to any advantage or profit to oneself. But the trial is not over.

Second Heavenly Council:
Satan's Second Challenge to Job's Integrity (2.1–6)

Again it came to pass on the day when the sons of God came to present themselves before Jehovah, that Satan came also among them to pres-

ent himself before Jehovah. ²And Jehovah said unto Satan, From whence comest thou? And Satan answered Jehovah, and said, From going to and fro in the earth, and from walking up and down in it. ³And Jehovah said unto Satan, Hast thou considered my servant Job? for [Or, that] there is none like him in the earth, a perfect and an upright man, one that feareth God, and turneth away from evil: and he still holdeth fast his integrity, although thou movedst me against him, to destroy him [Heb. *to swallow him up*] without cause. ⁴And Satan answered Jehovah, and said, Skin for skin, yea, all that a man hath will he give for his life. ⁵But put forth thy hand now, and touch his bone and his flesh, and he will renounce thee to thy face. ⁶And Jehovah said unto Satan, Behold, he is in thy hand; only spare his life.

1. Second Presentation Before Jehovah (1–2), as in 1.6–7.

2. Jehovah's Evaluation of Job Updated (3), as before (1.8) but with an addition: "…and he still holds fast his integrity," in spite of the fact that Satan had moved God against him, "to destroy him without cause."

3. Satan's Second Proposal (4–5) is expressed in a proverb, the meaning of which is uncertain. The context indicates the general sense: Satan still does not admit the genuineness of Job's piety. The trial has not gone deep enough, he says. If the trial went beyond the taking away of the rewards, if it actually touched the man himself, Satan was sure Job would renounce God. Observe that in this case more is to be done than taking away God's gifts. Hostile action is to be taken against the man himself.

4. Permission Granted (6). The trial could not have gone beyond this, despite the limitation: "only spare his life." Taking Job's life would not have increased the trial, for Job considered that he would be better off dead (ch 3). On the other hand, death would have ended the trial.

Additional Definition of the Issue Provided by the Second Challenge

A man might serve God for the reward. When the reward is taken away, will he then serve God? Job has met this test. One might assume that the genuineness of his piety has been established beyond question. But another reason a man might serve God is out of fear of what God might do to him if he does not. But let him be struck such a blow that he feels nothing more could be done—*i.e.*, that even death or hell could be no worse. Will he then serve God? In that case, piety is stripped down to its bare essence with no possibility of ulterior motives left to becloud the issue. If man then serves God, it will be simply and solely because God is God, *i.e.*, out of a genuine reverence for God, an acknowledgment of who God is.

That is the question with which Job is to be confronted: Will he serve God simply and solely because God is God? We shall see, not only in his initial reaction but in his fuller ruminations (or agonizing) over this issue in the debate that follows, what answer he will give to this question.

In the process of debating his affliction with his friends, Job must turn this question all around in his mind, examining the issue from every angle, considering every possibility. The alternatives include the possibilities that God may be powerless (or limited in power) or evil—in either case, unworthy of genuine worship with the mind. We will go over the ground with Job and, at the end of the trial, be left shouting with joy as Job emerges triumphant from such a trial; and what a lesson about God we shall have learned.

Questions to Consider: Is this the essence of real faith, the thing God must find out about a person, the basis on which that person will be judged? And, further, is every person tested somehow to that extent, so that it becomes clear that he or she will serve God simply because God is God?

Perhaps we can only speculate. I can think of no evidence in scripture that speaks directly to the last question. It may not be necessary for every person to be tested to the extent Job was. But one point cannot be missed. The Book of Job certainly teaches that God is worthy to be served if for no other reason than that he is God, even if we must serve him without reward and even if we feel we have nothing to lose by not serving him. In that way the book serves to prepare us for that possible eventuality and encourages us to hold on to God even if we must suffer as Job did.

Job's Reaction to the Additional Blow (2.7–10)

7So Satan went forth from the presence of Jehovah, and smote Job with sore boils from the sole of his foot unto his crown. 8And he took him a potsherd to scrape himself therewith; and he sat among the ashes. 9Then said his wife unto him, Dost thou still hold fast thine integrity? renounce God, and die. 10But he said unto her, Thou speakest as one of the foolish [Or, impious] women speaketh. What? shall we receive good at the hand of God, and shall we not receive evil? In all this did not Job sin with his lips.

1. Job's Affliction (7). Speculation about Job's disease is useless. The symptoms can, however, be summarized from the book itself.

2. Job on the Ash Heap (8). A piece of broken pottery is used by Job to scrape himself. The scraping may be due to itching. The ash heap or dung hill has been described by Wetzstein in Delitzsch. Basically Job is an outcast at this point.

3. Job's Wife (9) has been spared, but she was no advantage to Job. She becomes the one who actually gives voice to Satan's temptation to renounce God (*cf.* 1.11; 2.5). Satan's skepticism is certainly justified in her case. Her answer to the question whether God is to be served unconditionally, without reserve, no matter what, is "No." She thinks Job will be better off to turn on God, bringing God's final blow upon himself and thus escape the suffering in death.

4. Job's Reaction (10). Still he will not criticize God or attribute anything unworthy to him. He will not say that God has acted unworthily or inappropriately.

Job's Three Friends (2.11–13)

¹¹Now when Job's three friends heard of all this evil that was come upon him, they came every one from his own place: Eliphaz the Temanite, and Bildad the Shuhite, and Zophar the Naamathite, and they made an appointment together to come to bemoan him and to comfort him. ¹²And when they lifted up their eyes afar off, and knew him not, they lifted up their voice, and wept; and they rent every one his robe, and sprinkled dust upon their heads toward heaven. ¹³So they sat down with him upon the ground seven days and seven nights, and none spake a word unto him: for they saw that his grief [Or, pain] was very great.

1. Purpose of Their Coming (11). They come as friends with kind intentions: "to sympathize with him and to comfort him." But as will soon be seen, their attempts to comfort Job are misguided and irrelevant; instead of receiving comfort from them, Job is antagonized.

The friends' getting word about Job's trouble and their arrangements to get together and go to him would take some time. So Job has been in this misery for some time when they arrive.

2. Initial Reaction to the Sight of Job (12). Like Jehovah's "servant" (Isa 52.14), Job's affliction has left him unrecognizable. At the sight they weep aloud and manifest their deep grief in the customary manner.

3. Week of Silence (13). They sit in silent sympathy. Perhaps there is simply nothing to say. Perhaps they can not be sure will would be welcome (*cf.* 4.2). Job is already suffering so much. They may think words will only increase his misery.

Job's Complaint: The Great "Why" (Job 3)

After this opened Job his mouth, and cursed his day. ²And Job answered and said:

³Let the day perish wherein I was born,
And the night which said, There is a man-child conceived.
⁴Let that day be darkness;
Let not God from above seek for it,
Neither let the light shine upon it.
⁵Let darkness and the shadow of death [Or, deep darkness (and so elsewhere)] claim it for their own;
Let a cloud dwell upon it;
Let all that maketh black the day terrify it.
⁶As for that night, let thick darkness seize upon it:
Let it not rejoice among the days of the year;
Let it not come into the number of the months..
⁷Lo, let that night be barren [Or, solitary];
Let no joyful voice come therein.
⁸Let them curse it that curse the day,
Who are ready [Or, skilful] to rouse up leviathan.
⁹Let the stars of the twilight thereof be dark:
Let it look for light, but have none;
Neither let it behold the eyelids of the morning:
¹⁰Because it shut not up the doors of my *mother's* womb,
Nor hid trouble from mine eyes.
¹¹Why died I not from the womb?
Why did I not give up the ghost when my mother bare me?
¹²Why did the knees receive me?
Or why the breast, that I should suck?
¹³For now should I have lain down and been quiet;
I should have slept; then had I been at rest,
¹⁴With kings and counsellors of the earth,
Who built up waste places [Or, built solitary piles] for themselves;
¹⁵Or with princes that had gold,
Who filled their houses with silver:
¹⁶Or as a hidden untimely birth I had not been,
As infants that never saw light.
¹⁷There the wicked cease from troubling [Or, raging];
And there the weary are at rest.
¹⁸There the prisoners are at ease together;
They hear not the voice of the taskmaster.
¹⁹The small and the great are there:

And the servant is free from his master.
²⁰Wherefore is light given to him that is in misery,
And life unto the bitter in soul;
²¹Who long [Heb. *wait*] for death, but it cometh not,
And dig for it more than for hid treasures;
²²Who rejoice exceedingly [or unto exultation],
And are glad, when they can find the grave?
²³*Why is light given* to a man whose way is hid,
And whom God hath hedged in?
²⁴For my sighing cometh before I eat [or, like my food],
And my groanings [Heb. *roarings*] are poured out like water.
²⁵For the thing which I fear cometh [or, the thing which I feared is come *etc.*]
upon me ,
And that which I am afraid of cometh unto me.
²⁶I am not at ease, neither am I quiet, neither have I rest;
But trouble cometh [or, was not at ease …yet trouble came].

Job's immediate reaction to the first trial is recorded by the author as a calm acceptance, and praise to the name of God. "Through all this Job did not sin nor did he blame (or ascribe unseemliness to) God" (1.20–22). His acceptance of the bad with the good continues after the second stage of the trial, in which he is personally afflicted. "In all this Job did not sin with his lips" (2.10). But those who take these evaluations as representing Job's final reaction are greatly mistaken. Otherwise, why the reproof of Job by Elihu, which stands uncorrected by any speaker or by the author of the book? And why is Job rebuked by Jehovah?

Under the pressures of the debate with his friends, added to the adversity itself, Job will sin; he will charge God with wrong; he will "sin with his lips." His initial outburst is not the worst complaint he will make but already involves a questioning of divine providence. Eliphaz will be alarmed into speaking out and will be fully justified in speaking a word of caution, which initiates the debate.

After a week, Job can bear the silence no more. He bursts out with a wish that he had never been born. He considers that he would be better off dead. He wonders why life is prolonged for such as he. His outburst, an expression of pent-up rage, is not explicitly a complaint against God, though it is certainly implied.

The speech has three parts:

1. A Curse Upon the Day of His Birth (3–10). Actually the night of his conception is included. Do not look for strict logic or rationality in this emotional outburst. The reason for the curse is finally stated in verse 10. It is, in effect, a wish that he had never been born.

2. The Wish for Death (11–19). As dark and gloomy as Sheol (the realm of the dead) is often portrayed in the Old Testament, it seems a state of existence greatly to be preferred to Job's present circumstances.

3. The Senselessness of Life in Misery (20–26). Why is life prolonged to those in such misery that they long for death? It seems to make no sense at all.

And so the discussion begins. Job's complaint opens a great debate in which this question is explored by the best that human wisdom could offer.

Debate: The Problem Addressed by Human Wisdom

Job 4–31

Seeing how much Job was suffering, Eliphaz and the other two friends sat silently with Job for a full week. But Eliphaz is shocked by Job's outburst and feels that he can remain silent no longer, even if Job's misery is thereby increased. Thus begins the discussion or debate between Job and his friends (chs 4–28). Each friend speaks and Job replies. The debate continues through three cycles of speeches, except that the third friend does not deliver a third speech.

Chapters 1–3 set the stage for the debate. The situation is this: A righteous man named Job—the best man on earth by God's own estimation—has been struck one blow after another, all with God's permission and approval. He is suffering so severely that he longs for death. But he is not told the reason. The reader has been given information that neither Job nor his friends have. The debate is a discussion of the issues that arise from this situation.

It is probably not just traditional philosophy, as held by Job and his friends, but the universal instinct of humanity that people who live righteously should prosper and people who live lawless, wicked lives should suffer the consequences. But that instinct is not always realized in actual fact, and, in fact, sometimes very good people experience very great affliction. The present debate deals with the situation that the best man on earth suffers as one might expect only the lawless and antisocial should suffer.

As Francis I. Anderson has written, Job makes two magnificent affirmations after being so cruelly afflicted (1.21 and 2.10). "Job believes that

God, as Sovereign, may give or retrieve His gifts at His pleasure (1.21b); He may send good or bad (2.10b). He is not accountable to any man for such actions." But the problem comes when the traditional and even instinctive philosophy is brought in to explain the case of Job, for it certainly does not fit the case of Job. The prologue has made that point very clear to the reader. But the participants in the debate are not privy to the look behind the scenes that has been disclosed to the reader. They must search for answers without the advantage of that information.

Job has posed the great question: "Why?" But neither Job nor his friends have the advantage of revelation from God. They look at the problem of human suffering from every angle that human wisdom can suggest. When they have said all they can say, a judgment is made on the debate in Chapter 28. Though man has shown great skill in his pursuit of the treasures of the earth, he has not been able to attain wisdom.

Historical First Round of Speeches (Job 4–14)

The starting point was Job's complaint that seemed to question divine providence and to reflect irreverence toward God. In the first round of speeches we shall find each of the friends in turn trying to teach Job about God. They consider that he needs to learn reverence toward God. Job! Who knows as much about God as any of them. The most pious man on earth must sit and listen to this elementary instruction. The friends make wonderful speeches, all completely irrelevant to the case. Job is outraged.

Eliphaz' First Speech (4–5)

Job's complaint shocks Eliphaz into speaking. Eliphaz does not regard Job as a sinner or godless man. He considers him a godly man who has fallen into sin, such as is characteristic of the entire human race. He considers Job's afflictions to be a chastisement intended to correct him. But Job should beware of "vexation." If he will only humbly submit to chastisement, seeking God with true repentance, he will be restored to the blessed life. Eliphaz' teaching is generally true but entirely irrelevant to Job's case, as we know from the prologue.

Eliphaz is sympathetic toward Job as he begins. His first speech is a genuine attempt to offer comfort.

Opening Attempt at Comfort (4.1–11)

Then answered Eliphaz the Temanite, and said,
²If one assay to commune with thee, wilt thou be grieved?
But who can withhold himself from speaking?
³Behold, thou hast instructed many,
And thou hast strengthened the weak hands.
⁴Thy words have upholden him that was falling,
And thou hast made firm the feeble [Heb. *bowing*] knees.
⁵But now it is come unto thee, and thou faintest [Or, art grieved];
It toucheth thee, and thou art troubled.
⁶Is not thy fear *of God* thy confidence,
And the integrity of thy ways thy hope?
⁷Remember, I pray thee, who *ever* perished, being innocent?
Or where were the upright cut off?
⁸According as I have seen, they that plow iniquity,
And sow trouble [Or, mischief], reap the same.
⁹By the breath of God they perish,
And by the blast of his anger are they consumed.
¹⁰The roaring of the lion, and the voice of the fierce lion,
And the teeth of the young lions, are broken.
¹¹The old lion perisheth for lack of prey,
And the whelps of the lioness are scattered abroad.

1. Opening Questions (2). ICC observes that almost every speech from the friends begins with a question. (Job 20.2 and 25.2 are exceptions.) Eliphaz is hesitant, almost apologetic. It seems hard to speak as he must to a man who is already suffering so much. But after Job's shocking outburst Eliphaz feels that he cannot hold back.

2. The Comforter of Others in Need of Comfort (3–5). Job has often been the comforter of others. But now that Job himself has been afflicted, the counsel he has often given to others seems to be of no use to him. Instead of taking comfort from his own words, he has fallen into despair. Eliphaz will try to help.

3. Comfort on the Ground of Job's Good Life (6–11). Eliphaz assumes that Job is a pious man. That is the very thing that should give him hope (6). He must remember that only the truly wicked people are cut off before their time (7–11). The kind of person Eliphaz has in mind is clear from verse 8—not merely those who have been tempted and fallen into sin, but those who make lawlessness their business: They "plow iniquity and sow trouble" as a farmer plows and sows his fields.

As Eliphaz continues, we shall see that he does not regard Job as such a man. But he does hold that no man is wholly righteous in God's eyes and is confident that Job has fallen into sin for which he is being chastised. However, the prologue has shown that even this does not meet Job's case.

Ferocious wicked persons such as Eliphaz has in mind are often compared to a lion (*cf.* Psa 17.12; 22.13, 21; 34.10; Prov 28.15). The destruction of the wicked is compared to the breaking up and dispersion of a den of lions (in 10f).

A Vision in the Night (4.12–21)

¹²Now a thing was secretly brought to me [Heb. *brought by stealth*],
And mine ear received a whisper thereof.
¹³In thoughts from the visions of the night,
When deep sleep falleth on men,
¹⁴Fear came upon me, and trembling,
Which made all my bones to shake.
¹⁵Then a spirit passed before [Or, a breath passed over] my face;
The hair of my flesh stood up.
¹⁶It stood still, but I could not discern the appearance thereof;
A form was before mine eyes:
There was silence, and I heard a voice [Or, I heard a still voice], *saying,*
¹⁷Shall mortal man be more just than God [Or, be just before God]?
Shall a man be more pure than his Maker [Or, be pure before his Maker]?
¹⁸Behold, he putteth no trust in his servants;
And his angels he chargeth with folly:
¹⁹How much more them that dwell in houses of clay,
Whose foundation is in the dust,
Who are crushed before [Or, like] the moth!
²⁰Betwixt morning and evening [Or, from morning to evening] they are destroyed [Heb. *broken in pieces*]:
They perish for ever without any regarding it.
²¹Is not their tent-cord plucked up within them? [Or, Is not their excellency which is in them removed?]
They die, and that without wisdom.

Many see this section as an explanation of the real cause of affliction—*i.e.*, man's sinfulness. But where is this connection made? The explanation offered below takes note of the fact that Eliphaz is concerned about the "vexation" (ASV) or "wrath" (KJV) Job expressed in chapter 3 (5.2). The passage is a warning to Job.

1. Source of Eliphaz' Message (12–16). Eliphaz describes the source of the message he puts before Job. It was revealed to him in a frightful dream or nightmare. When the revelation is explained as below (*i.e.*, actually as a warning), the frightfulness with which it came is understandable.

2. Content of This Revelation (17–21): "Shall mortal man be more just than God? *etc.*" Job's questioning of divine providence (in ch 3) would seem to imply this. *More just than God* "is the meaning ordinarily conveyed by this (Hebrew) construction, the normal device for expressing the comparative sense" (Pope), and, despite the arguments of Pope and other scholars, I do not believe this translation is against the context. True, this dream may have come in the past, before Job's complaint (ch 3). But Eliphaz himself might well have had occasion in the past to question divine providence, and such ruminations can easily have produced such a dream. Eliphaz now recalls the message of the dream after hearing Job's complaint, which seems to sit in judgment on divine providence.

The message of the dream and the message Eliphaz thinks Job needs to hear is that mortal man is certainly not more righteous than God (17). Furthermore, in answer to Job's repeated "why" (3.11f, 20ff), Eliphaz continues: It is not surprising if the workings of divine providence are kept secret from mankind. God puts no trust in even heavenly ministers, such as the angels, whom he charges with folly (18) and, therefore, does not disclose all his secrets to them. How much more shall the lower creatures, whose existence is so lowly and fragile (as described in 19–21), be charged with folly. Mankind lives only a short time and dies without gaining wisdom. If God does not take the angels into his confidence, it is certainly not surprising that he leaves mere human beings in the dark on the secrets of his providence. It is certainly inappropriate for such puny creatures to criticize the arrangements of divine providence simply because they do not understand them.

Warning Against Bitter Resentment (5.1–7)

Call now; is there any that will answer thee?
And to which of the holy ones wilt thou turn?
²For vexation killeth the foolish man,
And jealousy [Or, indignation] slayeth the silly one.
³I have seen the foolish taking root:
But suddenly I cursed his habitation.
⁴His children are far from safety,

And they are crushed in the gate,
Neither is there any to deliver them:
⁵Whose harvest the hungry eateth up,
And taketh it even out of the thorns;
And the snare gapeth for [Acc. to Vulg., *the thirsty swallow up*] their
    substance.
⁶For affliction [Or, iniquity: See 4.8] cometh not forth from the dust,
Neither doth trouble spring out of the ground;
⁷But man is born unto trouble,
As the sparks [Heb. *the sons of flame* or *of lightning*] fly upward.

The general teaching set forth in this passage is now specifically applied to Job in a warning against murmuring and complaining. Eliphaz is shocked by Job's complaint (ch 3). He is afraid for Job; hence the warning.

1. Nowhere to Turn (1). Job has cried out. But to whom? Not to God (8), as Eliphaz sees it. His cry is a complaint against the arrangements of divine providence. To whom can he turn and find someone to take his part in such a complaint? He has nowhere to turn—certainly not to the "holy ones" (= angels).

2. Warning Against Vexation (2). "Vexation" is bitter resentment of treatment regarded as unmerited or unjust. Such an outcry, says Eliphaz, can bring no help (1). Instead, "vexation kills the foolish man, and jealousy (or indignation, margin) slays the silly one." Eliphaz warns that Job is talking like a foolish man, and thereby places himself in jeopardy.

3. Warning Supported by Observation (3–5). Eliphaz proves what is said in verse 2 by his own observation of the end to which a fool is brought by vexation.

4. Further Support for the Warning Against Vexation (6–7). After all, says Eliphaz, affliction and trouble do not spring up out of the ground like weeds. It is just part of the human experience, as much so as it is the nature of sparks to fly upward from a fire. The implication seems to be: Take note of this fact and do not let vexation destroy you.

Advice to Job: "Seek God" (5.8–16)

⁸But as for me, I would seek unto God,
And unto God would I commit my cause;
⁹Who doeth great things and unsearchable,
Marvellous things without number:
¹⁰Who giveth rain upon the earth,

And sendeth waters upon the fields;
¹¹So that he setteth up on high those that are low,
And those that mourn are exalted to safety.
¹²He frustrateth the devices of the crafty,
So that their hands cannot perform their enterprise [Or, can perform
  nothing of worth].
¹³He taketh the wise in their own craftiness;
And the counsel of the cunning is carried headlong.
¹⁴They meet with darkness in the day-time,
And grope at noonday as in the night.
¹⁵But he saveth from the sword of their mouth [Heb. *out of their mouth*],
Even the needy from the hand of the mighty.
¹⁶So the poor hath hope,
And iniquity stoppeth her mouth.

1. Eliphaz in Job's Place (8). This passage stands in sharp contrast to the preceding: "But as for me, *etc.*" In your place, says Eliphaz to Job, instead of voicing such bitter resentment "I would seek God" and "commit my cause" to him.

2. Justification of This Advice (9–16). The remainder of the passage is a description of God's marvelous works, which has the effect of supplying a reason for the advice given. The reason it is wise to turn to God is because of the wonderful works he is known to do. These wonderful works show what can be expected from him.

Blessings of Divine Chastening (5.17–27)

¹⁷Behold, happy is the man whom God correcteth [Or, *reproveth*]:
Therefore despise not thou the chastening of the Almighty.
¹⁸For he maketh sore, and bindeth up;
He woundeth, and his hands make whole.
¹⁹He will deliver thee in six troubles;
Yea, in seven there shall no evil touch thee.
²⁰In famine he will redeem thee from death;
And in war from the power of the sword.
²¹Thou shalt be hid from the scourge of the tongue;
Neither shalt thou be afraid of destruction when it cometh.
²²At destruction and dearth thou shalt laugh;
Neither shalt thou be afraid of the beasts of the earth.
²³For thou shalt be in league with the stones of the field;
And the beasts of the field shall be at peace with thee.

²⁴And thou shalt know that thy tent is in peace;
And thou shalt visit thy fold [Or, habitation], and shalt miss nothing
   [Or, shalt not err].
²⁵Thou shalt know also that thy seed shall be great,
And thine offspring as the grass of the earth.
²⁶Thou shalt come to thy grave in a full age,
Like as a shock of grain cometh in in its season.
²⁷Lo this, we have searched it, so it is;
Hear it, and know thou it for thy good [Heb. *for thyself*].

1. Eliphaz' Counsel (17). Now we see how Eliphaz views Job. As we have seen (*cf.* 4.1–11) he does not view Job as a wicked man. He sees him as a pious man who has fallen into sin. His suffering is a divine chastening, an attempt to correct Job and to turn him to the right way. Eliphaz' counsel is to submit to the divine chastisement, not to rebel against it.

2. The Blessed Life to Follow (18–26). These blessings will follow once Job submits to correction.

3. Final Assurance and Admonition (27). Eliphaz has no doubt that he has spoken the truth. "We have searched it." This is what we have found to be the truth. Job, therefore, should pay strict attention for his own good.

Evaluation of Eliphaz's Speech

Eliphaz says some beautiful things. Davidson calls his speech "one of the masterpieces of the Book." But there are two faults:

1. A Lack of Sympathy. Eliphaz comes across as a theologian who is so absorbed in ideas—what he understands to be the truth—that he is not touched by the feeling of Job's infirmities. He has no feeling for the extreme suffering which has wrung the outburst from Job. Consider especially his promise of future offspring (5.25), as though the loss of Job's earlier children was nothing—something easily forgotten. Eliphaz is simply off in another world so far as Job was concerned. He appears cold and without compassion.

2. Irrelevance. The speech is generally true. But we know from the prologue that it is beside the point. Eliphaz's speech simply flies off past the mark. Therefore, instead of comforting Job, it drives him into further rage.

Job's Reply to Eliphaz (6–7)

Defense of His Bitter Complaint (6.1–7)

Then Job answered and said,
²Oh that my vexation were but weighed,
And all my calamity laid in the balances!
³For now it would be heavier than the sand of the seas:
Therefore have my words been rash.
⁴For the arrows of the Almighty are within me,
The poison whereof my spirit drinketh up:
The terrors of God do set themselves in array against me.
⁵Doth the wild ass bray when he hath grass?
Or loweth the ox over his fodder?
⁶Can that which hath no savor be eaten without salt?
Or is there any taste in the white of an egg [Or, the juice of purslain]?
⁷My soul refuseth to touch *them*;
They are as loathsome food to me. [Or, *What things* my soul refused to touch,
these are as my loathsome food.]

Job lights on one word Eliphaz used, the word "vexation", and the warning that such bitterness is characteristic of "the foolish man" and the cause of his destruction (5.2). Job is deeply wounded by the implications and begins by addressing this warning. He defends his rash words on the ground of the greatness of his suffering.

1. Job's Rash Words Justified by the Greatness of His Suffering (1–4). "Vexation" alludes to Eliphaz's warning (5.2) and refers to Job's complaint (ch 3). The word refers to bitter resentment of treatment regarded as undeserved and unjust. But here "vexation" must refer to the thing that vexes Job, that causes his resentment, rather than the bitter resentment itself. For it is Job's vexation that is to be weighed, but not in comparison with his "calamity" in the next line. Rather it is synonymous with "calamity." Then the "it" spoken of in 3a refers back to his affliction, thought of first as "vexation," then as "calamity."

Job expresses the wish that his vexation (in the sense explained above) might be weighed along with the calamity that has befallen him. Then the rashness of his words would be understood (2f).

Further explanation of the weight of Job's suffering is added in verse 4. Job explicitly names God as the source of his afflictions. Like an enemy, the Almighty has shot his poison arrows into me, and his terrors are arrayed against me (unjustifiably, Job feels). He complains because his spirit has drunk up the Lord's poison.

2. Job's Vexation Compared to the Discontent of One Without Satisfying Food (5–7). Job's outcry is like that of the lower animals (wild donkey, ox) who do not cry out with discontent when their need for satisfying food has been met (5). So Job is like someone with nothing fit to eat. His afflictions, coming upon him without explanation, are certainly unsatisfying like tasteless and even repulsive food (6–7).

Compare the repeated "why" in chapter 3, verses 11, 12, 20–23. An explanation would be like salt, making afflictions easier to take.

Renewal of the Wish for Death (6.8–13)

⁸Oh that I might have my request;
And that God would grant *me* the thing that I long for!
⁹Even that it would please God to crush me;
That he would let loose his hand, and cut me off!
¹⁰And be it still my consolation,
Yea [Or, Though I shrink back], let me exult [Or, harden myself] in pain that
    spareth not [Or, though he spare not],
That I have not denied [Or, concealed] the words of the Holy One.
¹¹What is my strength, that I should wait?
And what is mine end, that I should be patient?
¹²Is my strength the strength of stones?
Or is my flesh of brass?
¹³Is it not that I have no help in me,
And that wisdom is driven quite from me?

1. The Longing for Death (8–10). Amidst suffering so great Job bursts forth with a renewal of his longing for death first expressed in chapter 3. He wishes God would restrain his hand no longer (*cf.* 2.6) but turn it loose in full force and strike him a death blow (9). The consolation Job wishes, confident that he has been faithful to the Holy One, is the unsparing pain that seeks to put an end to his life (10).

2. Job's Resources Insufficient (11–13). Eliphaz tried to encourage Job with the bright prospects that would be his if he received his chastisement in the proper spirit (5.17–27). Job replies that he is without strength to endure or hope to bolster his spirits and help him last it out (11). A man of flesh, he does not have the strength of stone or brass (12). Nor does he have the inner resources any more than the physical strength to endure such trial (13). Hence his despair!

Disappointment at the Failure of His Friends (6.14–23)

¹⁴To him that is ready to faint kindness *should be showed* from his friend;
Even to him that forsaketh [Or, Else might he forsake; or, But he
    forsaketh] the fear of the Almighty.
¹⁵My brethren have dealt deceitfully as a brook,
As the channel of brooks that pass away;
¹⁶Which are black by reason of the ice,
And wherein the snow hideth itself:
¹⁷What time they wax warm [Or shrink], they vanish;
When it is hot, they are consumed out of their place.
¹⁸The caravans *that travel* by the way of them turn aside [Or, The paths of
    their way are turned aside];
They go up into the waste, and perish.
¹⁹The caravans of Tema looked,
The companies of Sheba waited for them.
²⁰They were put to shame because they had hoped;
They came thither, and were confounded.
²¹For now ye are nothing [Another reading is, *are like thereto*];
Ye see a terror, and are afraid.
²²Did I say, Give unto me?
Or, Offer a present for me of your substance?
²³Or, Deliver me from the adversary's hand?
Or, Redeem me from the hand of the oppressors?

1. Expectation of a Friend (14). One who is "ready to faint" should be able to expect kindness from a friend, even though he seems in danger of falling away from God, or with ASV margin (and NASB text): or else he might fall away.

2. Failure of the Friends (15–21). Job feels his friends have miserably failed him. They are like the wadis so common in Syria-Palestine—overflowing with water after the snow melts or in the rainy season, but in the summer's heat quickly drying up, disappointing the caravans that come to them looking for refreshment (15–20). So with Job's friends (21). They had come to comfort him but see a "terror," referring to Job's frightful condition, and are afraid, incapable of offering comfort.

3. No Great Favor Asked (22–23). Job has asked nothing of his friends— no great expenditure of money or act of power. He only hopes for the kindness one has every right to expect from a friend (*cf.* 14).

Challenge to the Friends (6.24–30)

²⁴Teach me, and I will hold my peace;
And cause me to understand wherein I have erred.
²⁵How forcible are words of uprightness!
But your reproof, what doth it reprove?
²⁶Do ye think to reprove words,
Seeing that the speeches of one that is desperate are as wind [Or, for the
    wind]?
²⁷Yea, ye would cast *lots* upon the fatherless,
And make merchandise of your friend.
²⁸Now therefore be pleased to look upon me;
For surely I shall not lie to your face [Or, And it will be evident   unto you
    if I lie].
²⁹Return, I pray you, let there be no injustice;
Yea, return again, my cause is righteous [Heb. *my righteousness is   in it*].
³⁰Is there injustice on my tongue?
Cannot my taste discern mischievous things?

1. Challenge to Convict Him of Sin (24–27). Eliphaz cautioned Job about his complaint (ch 3), which sounded to Eliphaz like the bitter resentment a foolish man might utter. Job replies that he would be silent if the friends would point out his guilt and prove that he deserved such suffering. Eliphaz has not directly charged Job with sin, but the implication throughout his speech was that Job's suffering is due to his sins (especially at 5.17). Job pleads wih his friends to point out his sins to him (24). Good honest words of reproof can be of powerful benefit; but what good are such insinuations as Eliphaz has made? (25). The friends seem to be merely reproving Job's "words" (referring to ch 3), as opposed to some sin in Job's life—not recognizing that the words of a desperate man are "as wind" or "for the wind" and not to be taken so seriously (26). If you would treat me as you have, Job says harshly, you would cast lots to decide who would take orphans as slaves to settle the debt left by their father (*cf.* 2 Kgs 4.1), or [perhaps?] sell out your friend (27). As Anderson comments, "Job can give as good as he gets."

2. Plea for Reconsideration (28–30). Job challenges his friends to look him in the eye and know that he is not lying to their faces when he claims to be innocent (28; *cf.* 10). He begs them to "turn" or "return," that is to "think again" (NEB); to come back and reconsider the case; or perhaps to return from the injustice of falsely accusing him. How important such a reconsideration of the case is to Job is explained by his claim: "my righteousness is in it" (literal translation in ASV margin), perhaps meaning his righteousness is at stake in this discussion or case.

The two questions of verse 30 are tantamount to a claim: "There is no injustice on my tongue," *i.e.* when he claims to be innocent or otherwise states his case (30a; *cf.* 28b). "My palate (the organ of taste) has the power to discern calamities" (30b). Job seems to have returned to the metaphor of 6f where he referred to his calamities as "tasteless," being as they were without explanation.

Complaint Addressed to God (7)

Job's consciousness of his innocence and his perceived personal injustice leads to a fresh outburst of despair at the human condition and the hopelessness of his plight. Perhaps from the beginning, certainly from verse 7 on to the end of the chapter, it is clear that Job has turned to God rather than to the friends with his complaint.

Misery of the Human Condition (7.1–10)

Is there not a warfare [Or, time of service] to man upon earth?
And are not his days like the days of a hireling?
²As a servant that earnestly desireth the shadow,
And as a hireling that looketh for his wages:
³So am I made to possess months of misery,
And wearisome nights are appointed to me.
⁴When I lie down, I say,
When shall I arise, and the night be gone?
And I am full of tossings to and fro unto the dawning of the day.
⁵My flesh is clothed with worms and clods of dust;
My skin closeth up, and breaketh out afresh [Or, is broken and become loathsome].
⁶My days are swifter than a weaver's shuttle,
And are spent without hope.
⁷Oh remember that my life is a breath:
Mine eye shall no more see good.
⁸The eye of him that seeth me shall behold me no more;
Thine eyes shall be upon me, but I shall not be.
⁹As the cloud is consumed and vanisheth away,
So he that goeth down to Sheol shall come up no more.
¹⁰He shall return no more to his house,
Neither shall his place know him any more.

1. Job's Miserable Existence (1–5). Job begins with reflection upon the hard struggle of mankind generally (1) but quickly moves on to his own particular struggle. As a servant who bears "the burden of the day and the scorching heat" (Matt 20.12) in the fields, eager for the shadow of evening, or a hired hand looking for his wages at the end of the day (Deut 24.15; Matt 20.8), such was Job's lot in life—"months of misery" and "wearisome nights" (2–3). He thinks especially of his long, pain-filled nights of restlessness (4) and the miserable condition of his body (5).

2. Brevity and Hopelessness of Life (6–10). Mindful that his days are passing swiftly and without hope (6), Job turns to God with a pathetic plea to remember how soon he will be gone (7). He has no hope of a return to prosperity (7b). He imagines that God may come looking for him, but it would be too late (8). He will have descended to the realm of the dead, never to return to his home (9–10).

Job's Complaint to God (7.11–21)

[11]Therefore I will not refrain my mouth;
I will speak in the anguish of my spirit;
I will complain in the bitterness of my soul.
[12]Am I a sea, or a sea-monster,
That thou settest a watch over me?
[13]When I say, My bed shall comfort me,
My couch shall ease my complaint;
[14]Then thou scarest me with dreams,
And terrifiest me through visions:
[15]So that my soul chooseth strangling,
And death rather than *these* my bones.
[16]I loathe *my life* [Or I waste away]; I would [Or, shall] not live alway:
Let me alone; for my days are vanity [Or, as a breath].
[17]What is man, that thou shouldest magnify him,
And that thou shouldest set thy mind upon him,
[18]And that thou shouldest visit him every morning,
And try him every moment?
[19]How long wilt thou not look away from me,
Nor let me alone till I swallow down my spittle?
[20]If I have sinned, what do I [Or, can I do] unto thee, O thou watcher [Or, preserver] of men?
Why hast thou set me as a mark for thee,
So that I am a burden to myself?

²¹**And why dost thou not pardon my transgression, and take away mine iniquity?**
For now shall I lie down in the dust;
And thou wilt seek me diligently, but I shall not be.

1. Job Determined to Give Voice to his Complaint (11). Eliphaz warned Job about the "vexation" expressed in his initial complaint (5.1–7 with ch 3) and bade him seek God (5.8) and submit to chastisement (5.17). But the case being as Job has described (7.1–10), he is determined to give full voice to his complaint (11; *cf.* 6.24). He will not be silenced by Eliphaz' warning.

2. Plea for Understanding: Why Such a Close Guard Over Him? (12–16). Job cries out for understanding. Why has he been treated this way? Is he a sea or a sea-monster that needed to be closely guarded lest it break out and cause some kind of great damage in the world? (12). This "guard" or "watch" which God keeps over him is then described. God simply will not leave him alone. He cannot even forget his troubles in sleep at night, for God terrifies him with nightmares, so that Job prefers death to life in his pain-filled body (13–15). Think, for example, of a guard over a prisoner, always standing ready to lash out with his whip. Job pleads with God to leave him in peace for the few days he has left (16).

3. So Much Attention Not Understandable in View of Man's Insignificance (17–19). Job cannot understand it. "What is man,…"—he seems so insignificant—that God should give such inordinate attention to testing him "every moment," not leaving him alone for an instant, not long enough even to swallow his spit? (17–19). Man does not seem to be that important. Job cannot understand it.

4. Such Treatment Not Understandable Even on the Assumption of Guilt (20–21). Job does not understand such treatment even on the assumption that he has sinned (20). How can the actions of a puny man affect one as great as God to the extent that he sets him up as a mark to strike and makes the man a burden to himself? Job is certainly no threat to overthrow the divine government (*cf.* 12).

Job's habit is regularly to approach God seeking forgiveness (*cf.* 1.5). He cannot understand why God does not just pardon his sin? (21a). Why wait till he dies and then come looking for him when it is too late? (21bc).

Job seems confident that God will eventually come looking for him. But nothing about the present situation makes any sense at all to him. Still it is to be noted that he does bring his honest complaint to the right person. Better this than a dishonest pretense of piety.

Furthermore, should Job not be such an honest man, one who speaks his mind and says what he really thinks, should he continue to give voice to pious platitudes along the lines of 1.20–22 and 2.10, then we who often feel the same perplexity and despair would have had no one to give voice to our complaints, and we would not have the benefit of the answers provided by this book. In other words, the Book of Job would not have been possible had Job simply put on his "church face" and pretended to be pious, never giving voice to the doubt and the despair he really felt. Job speaks for all who experience these things. Remember this thought as you make your way through this book and find Job's complaints growing in irreverence, even as he struggles to hold on to his faith.

Bildad's First Speech:
A Speech in Defense of the Justice of God (8)

Bildad passes over Job's defense of his bitter outcry (6.2–7) and his attack upon his friends (6.14–23). He ignores Job's challenge to teach him and show him his error (6.24–30). Job has stubbornly refused to be silenced by Eliphaz' warning about "vexation." His reply to Eliphaz concludes with an assertion of determination not to be silenced, but rather, to continue his complaint about the treatment he has received from God, for this treatment makes no sense, no matter how one looks at it (7.11–21). So Bildad passes over a great deal in order to come directly to the point he no doubt considers the most serious issue, or perhaps the real issue: the justice of God.

As Bildad sees the matter, Job's complaint to God, which includes the miserable lot of mankind in general and then his own treatment at the hands of God in particular, has called in question the justice of God. His speech is a strong assertion of God's justice (3). The undergirding principle is that God will always do right, which is to say that the godless person will be brought to nothing (11–19), while a pious person can expect far different treatment from God (20–22).

The Implications of Job's Speech Directly Addressed (8.1–7)

Then answered Bildad the Shuhite, and said,
²How long wilt thou speak these things?
And *how long* shall the words of thy mouth be *like* a mighty wind?
³Doth God pervert justice?

Or doth the Almighty pervert righteousness?
⁴If thy children have sinned against him,
And he hath delivered them into the hand of their transgression [Or, If thy
    chilldren sinned …he delivereth *etc.*];
⁵If thou wouldest seek diligently unto God,
And make thy supplication to the Almighty;
⁶If thou wert pure and upright:
Surely now he would awake for thee,
And make the habitation of thy righteousness prosperous.
⁷And though thy beginning was small,
Yet thy latter end would greatly increase.

1. The Implication of Injustice in God (2–3). The opening questions are best understood in reference to 6.26 and 7.11. Eliphaz has not pointed out Job's error, except to express alarm at his complaint (ch 3). Eliphaz reproves Job's "words," not understanding that the words of a man in desperate circumstances are like the blowing of the wind and not to be taken so seriously, as though his words are the best indicator of his character (6.26). Job feels he has good reason to complain of his lot and so is determined not to hold back, but to give expression to his complaint (7.11).

Bildad begins with an expression of impatience at Job's words. How long, asks Bildad, is this mighty wind going to blow? (2). Job's complaint implies the inconceivable—that the Almighty would pervert justice (3), in this case, pouring out upon Job suffering that he does not deserve. How long, Bildad asks, will Job continue to spue out these complaints which have such serious implications?

2. Encouragement to Seek God (4–7). Bildad seems to be making a genuine effort at comfort. It being inconceivable that God would pervert justice, Job's children (*cf.* 1.18f) must surely, therefore, have sinned against God and been punished for their transgression (4). Job, on the other hand, is still alive, and so can still be hopeful with regard to his future (5–7). If he would only seek God in prayer, providing of course that he is "pure and upright," God would surely respond by restoring his prosperity.

Bildad's "comfort," therefore, is founded upon the assumption that the righteous can always expect to prosper and that suffering is always due to sin in one's life. It was simply inconceivable to him that one might be "pure and upright" and still suffer such affliction as had come upon Job.

Recommendation: Consult the Wisdom of the Ancients (8.8–10)

⁸For inquire, I pray thee, of the former age,
And apply thyself to that which their fathers have searched out:
⁹(For we are but of yesterday, and know nothing,
Because our days upon earth are a shadow);
¹⁰Shall not they teach thee, and tell thee,
And utter words out of their heart?

Bildad's position (4–7) is supported by an appeal to the wisdom of former generations (8–10), as Eliphaz founded his warning to Job upon a revelation received in a dream (4.12–21). Our lives are so short that we do not have time to learn anything, Bildad argues. So he recommends that Job turn to the cumulative wisdom of the ancients—the truth learned by the former age or generation, and their fathers. Consult these former generations. Let them teach you.

The Teaching of the Ancients Summarized by Bildad (8.11–22)

¹¹Can the rush [Or, papyrus] grow up without mire?
Can the flag [Or, reed-grass] grow without water?
¹²Whilst it is yet in its greenness, *and* not cut down,
It withereth before any *other* herb.
¹³So are the paths of all that forget God;
And the hope of the godless man shall perish:
¹⁴Whose confidence shall break in sunder [Or, be cut off],
And whose trust is a spider's web [Heb. *house*].
¹⁵He shall lean upon his house, but it shall not stand:
He shall hold fast thereby, but it shall not endure.
¹⁶He is green before the sun,
And his shoots go forth over his garden.
¹⁷His roots are wrapped about the *stone* -heap [Or, beside the spring],
He beholdeth the place of stones.
¹⁸If he be destroyed from his place,
Then it shall deny him, *saying*, I have not seen thee.
¹⁹Behold, this is the joy of his way;
And out of the earth [Or, dust] shall others spring.
²⁰Behold, God will not cast away a perfect man,
Neither will he uphold the evil-doers.
²¹He will yet fill [Or, Till he fill] thy mouth with laughter,
And thy lips with shouting.
²²They that hate thee shall be clothed with shame;
And the tent of the wicked shall be no more.

1. The Destiny of the Godless (11–19). Bildad summarizes the teaching of the ancients in his own words. He compares the paths of those who endeavor to live without God to the papyrus plant or reed-grass without the water that is essential to their well-being. As these quickly wither without water, so the hope of the godless man perishes (11–13). All that he puts confidence in fails him (14–15).

The figure changes in verses 16–19. The godless man is like a plant that seems to spread and prosper but then is destroyed so completely as not to leave any sign that it was ever there (16–18), and others spring up to take its place (19).

2. Prospects of the Man of Integrity (20–22). In a concluding summary, Bildad repeats his general principle (20) on the ground of which he holds out happy prospects for Job's recovery (21)—provided of course that Job heeds his suggestion to seek God through prayer (5–7)—while Job's enemies, which he identifies with the wicked, reach an unhappy end (22).

Evaluation and Summary

Bildad is not hostile toward Job. He does his best to provide some comfort for Job. He no doubt fully expects Job to be encouraged by his remarks. The trouble is that Job has already done all that Bildad suggests. He was a man who seeks after God continually (5–7 with 1.1–5). He is just such a man of integrity as Bildad describes (20a with ch 1) with assurances that such a man will have a joyful life (20–22). Yet Job's life is not joyful. He is suffering and his life is miserable. So Bildad's speech flies wide of the mark. It has no comfort for a man in Job's position. It can only aggravate Job's misery, for he is experiencing the lot in life which one expects a wicked man to have.

Bildad's theology has no place for a suffering righteous man like Job. According to Bildad, one is either a righteous man who can expect to prosper at the hand of God, or a godless man who has no hope of enduring prosperity. Were the truth of Job's case to be disclosed to Bildad, on the basis of his position he would have to conclude that God is unjust. One need not be a prophet to predict that those who hold this position will eventually be forced to accuse Job of great sins. It is either accuse Job of sin or accuse God of injustice. Thus the friends are caught on the horns of a dilemma, and their position allows no escape.

Job's Reply to Bildad (9–10)

Part One: The Problem of Establishing One's Case in the Presence of God (9)

The Problem Stated (9.1–2)

Then Job answered and said,
²Of a truth I know that it is so:
But [Or, For] how can man be just with [Or, before] God?

Job admits the truth set forth by Bildad with regard to the righteousness of God (summarized in 8.3). But the problem is: How can a man be just or righteous (*i.e.*, in the right) with God? This question sets forth the theme developed throughout chapter 9 and must be understood in light of the whole development of thought in this chapter.

The point of the question in its context is this: Suppose a man has a complaint or a quarrel with God, as Job does (see 27). Suppose he feels that he has been mistreated, that God has brought upon him affliction which he does not deserve; how could he possibly go before God and establish his case in the presence of God? The law of Moses makes provision for controversy between men to be brought before judges and decided in court (Deut 25.1). But what if one's complaint is against God? How can he establish his case and prove the justice of his cause?

That is exactly the problem, as Job sees it. According to Bildad, God can never be accused of injustice. He would never mete out affliction upon one who does not deserve it. Yet, as Job perceives the matter, and as we know from the prologue, great suffering has been brought upon a man who does not deserve it. God seems to be treating Job as one would expect only the worst sinners to be treated. So the problem is: In such a case, how can a man go before God, establish his innocence, and argue that a great miscarriage of justice has taken place?

The Problem of Successful Argument with an Infinite God (9.3–10)

³If he be pleased to contend with him,
He cannot answer him one of a thousand [Or, If one should desire… he could not, *etc.*].
⁴*He is* wise in heart, and mighty in strength:
Who hath hardened himself against him, and prospered?—
⁵*Him* that removeth the mountains, and they know it not,

When he overturneth them in his anger;
⁶That shaketh the earth out of its place,
And the pillars thereof tremble;
⁷That commandeth the sun, and it riseth not,
And sealeth up the stars;
⁸That alone stretcheth out the heavens,
And treadeth upon the waves [Heb. *high places*] of the sea;
⁹That maketh the Bear, Orion, and the Pleiades,
And the chambers of the south;
¹⁰That doeth great things past finding out,
Yea, marvellous things without number.

Suppose, says Job, one wanted to "contend," "dispute" or argue his case
with God. The Hebrew verb means to strive or contend, with applications
ranging from bodily striving (as in Exod 21.18; Deut 33.7; Jdg 11.25) to a
striving with words (as here) and specifically of disputing a case in court.
Suppose someone should want to take his case with God to court and try
to prove his innocence in a lawsuit. Job is certain that a man would be no
match for God, no matter the merits of his case. God could easily overwhelm him with questions that he could not answer (3).

The remainder of this passage (4–10) is descriptive of God, his superior
wisdom and power as manifested in his works. The description serves to
reinforce Job's position with regard to the hopelessness of successful controversy with God. The question in 4b is the key to the point: Who has
ever come up against God and prospered? A man would have no chance
of successful controversy with such a superior being as God.

Problems of Contending with God (9.11–20)

¹¹Lo, he goeth by me, and I see him not:
He passeth on also, but I perceive him not.
¹²Behold, he seizeth *the prey*, who can hinder him [Or, turn him back]?
Who will say unto him, What doest thou?
¹³God will not withdraw his anger;
The helpers of Rahab [Or, arrogancy: See Isa 2.7.] do [Or, did] stoop under him.
¹⁴How much less shall I answer him,
And choose out my words *to reason* with him?
¹⁵Whom, though I were righteous, yet would I not answer;
I would make supplication to my judge.
¹⁶If I had called, and he had answered me,
Yet would I not believe that he hearkened unto my voice.

¹⁷For he [Heb. *He who*] breaketh me with a tempest,
And multiplieth my wounds without cause.
¹⁸He will not suffer me to take my breath,
But filleth me with bitterness.
¹⁹If *we speak* of strength, lo, *he is* mighty!
And if of justice, Who, *saith he*, will summon me? [Or, Lo, *here am I,*
     saith he; and if of judgment, Who *etc.*]
²⁰Though I be righteous, mine own mouth shall condemn me:
Though I be perfect, it [Or, he] shall prove me perverse.

God passes by me, says Job, though I do not see him (11). He uses his vast power as he pleases, and none can either prevent it or even call him to account (12). Furthermore, when God unleashes his anger without relenting, even such superior beings as "the helpers of Rahab" can only cower beneath him (13). What chance then would the puny Job have in controversy with God? (14). He would neither be able to respond to his questions nor to prepare a case to reason with him in a matter of controversy.

Even if in the right, Job thinks he would be overwhelmed by divine power, unable to establish his case, and having to beg his judge for mercy rather than being vindicated (15).

Even if God responded to Job's call (evidently for a hearing of the case), Job says he would not believe that God had actually paid attention to him (16). The reason is set forth in verses 17 and 18. Such a response would be so inconsistent with God's present treatment of him, and that "without cause."

Verse 19 seems to give further reason why Job finds a divine response to his call for a hearing so incredible—God's superiority to any challenge no matter what the nature of the question at issue. If it is a question of strength, God is mighty! …much stronger than any opponent. If, on the other hand, it is a question of legal action to determine what is right or who is in the right, who can bring him into court?

Before such superior power, even if in the right, Job would not be able to make his case but would botch the job and be condemned by his own mouth (20).

The Problem of Moral Indifference (9.21–24)

²¹I am perfect; I regard not myself;
I despise my life. [Or, Though I be perfect, I will not regard *etc.*]
²²It is all one; therefore I say,
He destroyeth the perfect and the wicked.

²³If the scourge slay suddenly,
He will mock at the trial [Or, calamity] of the innocent.
²⁴The earth is given into the hand of the wicked;
He covereth the faces of the judges thereof:
If *it be* not *he*, who then is it?

Job began this speech by conceding the truth of Bildad's position about the discriminating righteousness of God (1a). But now he reverses himself and directly denies Bildad's contention. His consideration of his own undeserved suffering and the problem of establishing the justice of his cause before God has provoked him to express his severest criticism of God so far and to challenge the moral government of the earth. Job is certainly on dangerous ground, and his expressions prove just how severe his faith is being tested at this point.

The feeling of helplessness at the impossibility of establishing his innocence before the Almighty drives Job to a reckless expression of despair. He asserts his innocence even though he thinks it may cost him his life (21). It makes no difference anyway, for God destroys righteous and wicked alike (22). When the scourge brings sudden death, God simply mocks at the plight of the innocent (23).

The moral government of the earth is directly challenged in verse 24. The earth is under the power or control of wicked people, perhaps the criminal element, so that they dominate; and the faces of the judges are covered, so they cannot see the right and give justice to the innocent. If God is not the one ultimately behind these conditions, then Job wants to know: Who is?

Futility of the Effort to Establish his Innocence (9.25–35)

²⁵Now my days are swifter than a post [Or, runner]:
They flee away, they see no good,
²⁶They are passed away as the swift ships [Or, ships of reed];
As the eagle that swoopeth on the prey.
²⁷If I say, I will forget my complaint,
I will put off my *sad* countenance, and be of good cheer [Heb. *brighten up*];
²⁸I am afraid of all my sorrows,
I know that thou wilt not hold me innocent.
²⁹I shall be condemned;
Why then do I labor in vain?
³⁰If I wash myself with snow water [Another reading is, *with snow*],

And make my hands never so clean [Heb. *cleanse my hands with lye*];
³¹Yet wilt thou plunge me in the ditch,
And mine own clothes shall abhor me.
³²For he is not a man, as I am, that I should answer him,
That we should come together in judgment.
³³There is no umpire betwixt us,
That might lay his hand upon us both.
³⁴Let him take his rod away from me,
And let not his terror make me afraid:
³⁵Then would I speak, and not fear him;
For I am not so in myself.

Job sees his life passing swiftly away (25–26). Three images illustrate the rapidity—the runner that carries messages; the ships of reed or "papyrus boats" (NIV) that move so rapidly across the water; the eagle swooping down upon its prey. Job's life will soon be over. So he considers that he will just forget his complaint, his quarrel with God, put off his sad appearance and put on a "happy face" (27). Perhaps Job thinks he can just put the problem out of his mind and trust that everything will turn out all right in the end. But he cannot take that view: His pains fill him with fear, for they are evidence to his mind that God will not find him innocent (28), evidence that he will be condemned as a wicked man (29a). His afflictions produce the conviction that God is determined to continue treating him as guilty, so that all his labor to present himself acceptable in the eyes of God will be as nothing (29b).

What is the use, when God is determined to find him guilty? No matter how much he may endeavor to be clean, he is convinced that God will not have it (30–31). Though he wash himself with the cleanest of water and the strongest detergent, God will just plunge him into a filthy pit or ditch, so that he is filthy still. His own clothes will abhor him, not wanting to be used to clothe such a filthy man.

Remember that it is the pain and suffering that makes him take this view of God (28a). The afflictions are God's witnesses against him (10.7; 16.8). If God were a man, Job could take him to court and answers these charges (*cf.* Deut 25.1). But he is not a man, and so cannot be met in such a deciding judgment (32). Hence, Job despairs of any chance of being found in the right.

Furthermore, Job bemoans the lack of an umpire or arbitrator—one who could decide the controversy between himself and God (33).

Job feels that he is being intimidated or bullied into silence by God with his superior power. If only, Job wishes, God will lay aside his rod and his awful majesty, Job will then not be afraid to plead his case before God (34–35). It is the terrorizing rod that makes Job afraid—not anything within himself (35b).

But under present circumstances, a man cannot argue and establish his case before God. He cannot be just with God (2). His labor toward that end is simply futile.

Part Two: The Pursuit of Understanding (10)

Out of his futility and despair Job said some terrible things about God in chapter 9. I have specially in mind his challenge to the way God rules the world (21–24) and, in his own case, the impossibility of getting justice despite his strong efforts to present himself acceptable to God (20–35). Such challenges to the divine government show us the toll Job's trials are taking on him and reveal the severity of the trial.

Job is being sorely tested, and, if we pay attention to his complaints, we shall realize that the actual physical suffering is the least of it. Far greater are the apparent spiritual implications of the affliction. God seems to be treating the best man on earth according to his own testimony as a sinner, and Job can see no way to get justice. God seems to be determined to treat him as a sinner despite all his efforts to be acceptable to God, and Job sees no way to get this grievance redressed.

But, on the other hand, notwithstanding his strong and daring words, Job does not turn his back on God. His faith does not crumble under the stress of the trial. He does not bid farewell to God as Satan thought he surely would. And he turns to God in Chapter 10 pleading: "Do not condemn me" (2) and begging God for some explanation of his plight. Chapter 10 is not the highest peak to which Job's faith will rise, but it is a beginning as he seeks understanding from God. And we shall see his faith continues to grow, even as the trial continues. This man is desperately trying to hold on to God.

The Reason for God's Hostility (10.1–7)

My soul is weary of my life;
I will give free course to my complaint;
I will speak in the bitterness of my soul.

²I will say unto God, Do not condemn me;
Show me wherefore thou contendest with me.
³Is it good unto thee that thou shouldest oppress,
That thou shouldest despise the work [Heb. *labor*] of thy hands,
And shine upon the counsel of the wicked?
⁴Hast thou eyes of flesh?
Or seest thou as man seeth?
⁵Are thy days as the days of man,
Or thy years as man's days,
⁶That thou inquirest after mine iniquity,
And searchest after my sin,
⁷Although thou knowest that I am not wicked,
And there is none that can deliver out of thy hand?

Weary of life, Job determines not to forget his complaint (9.27), nor to restrain his words, but rather boldly to give full expression to his complaint (1). Though in the previous chapter he expressed the conviction that he would be condemned no matter what he did (20, 29), he now appeals to God: "Do not condemn me," but show me the reason you have taken such a hostile stand toward me (2). The Hebrew verb, which means to strive or contend, is the same word we found in 9.3. As we saw there, its application ranges from actual bodily struggle to striving by means of words. Here the reference is to the afflictions God has brought on Job, in which he seems to be striving or contending with Job. Why, asks Job?

Job's mind seems to race, considering every explanation he can imagine (3–7). First: "Is it good (*i.e.*, beneficial, advantageous, profitable or fitting) to you that you should oppress and despise the work of your hands, and, in the meantime, shine (*i.e.*, look with favor) upon the counsel of the wicked?" (3). The counsel of the wicked is explained by 21.14–16 and 22.15–18. The wicked are those who repudiate God and think there is no profit in serving him. God's treatment of such a man as Job, while permitting the earth to fall under the control of the wicked, seems to favor the philosophy of the wicked. Has God found that to be good? Can that be the reason for Job's afflictions?

Second: "Do you have eyes of flesh? Or see as man sees?" *i.e.*, Are you as subject to error as man is and, consequently, mistaking the innocent for the guilty? (4).

Third: Are you as shortlived as man, so that you must relentlessly pursue my guilt, lest I outlive you and escape your justice? You surely know that I am innocent and furthermore that I am incapable of escaping your power (5–7).

The added words in verse 7 seem to dismiss the second and third proposals. In fact none of these possible explanations of God's hostility toward Job are anything but absurd. Yet the real reason is beyond the power of Job's mind. He begs God for an explanation. As I have suggested, even despite the hard sayings of chapter 9, Job is desperately trying to hold on to God.

God's Imagined Secret Purpose with Regard to Job (10.8–17)

⁸Thy hands have framed me and fashioned me
Together round about; yet thou dost destroy me.
⁹Remember, I beseech thee, that thou hast fashioned me as clay;
And wilt thou bring me into dust again?
¹⁰Hast thou not poured me out as milk,
And curdled me like cheese?
¹¹Thou hast clothed me with skin and flesh,
And knit me together with bones and sinews.
¹²Thou hast granted me life and lovingkindness;
And thy visitation [Or, care] hath preserved my spirit.
¹³Yet these things thou didst hide in thy heart;
I know that this is with thee:
¹⁴If I sin, then thou markest me,
And thou wilt not acquit me from mine iniquity.
¹⁵If I be wicked, woe unto me;
And if I be righteous, yet shall I not lift up my head;
Being filled with ignominy [Or, I am filled with ignominy, but look thou …for
  it increaseth: thou *etc.*],
And looking upon mine affliction.
¹⁶And if *my head* exalt itself, thou huntest me as a lion;
And again thou showest thyself marvellous upon me.
¹⁷Thou renewest thy witnesses against me,
And increasest thine indignation upon me:
Changes and warfare are with me [Or, Host after host is against me].

Job cannot figure it out. As incredible as it seems, Job thinks it must be true, that God has gone to the trouble of creating him only to destroy him and reduce him once again to dust (8–9). The elaboration of the way God has fashioned Job (10–12) covers the whole ground of formation in the womb (10) to the care given after birth (12).

All the while God is taking such care to form and bless him, Job imagines that God must have entertained the secred purpose (13) that is explained in verses 14–17. It is a plan to the effect that if Job fell into sin God would be watching and would not acquit him of guilt (14)—*i.e.*, not forgive him, but continue to hold him guilty.

In fact, it appears to Job that God has planned not to permit him to rise, no matter whether he is wicked or righteous (15). God will hunt him down as a lion seeks its prey and manifest his marvelous power against him (16).

The reason Job thinks God has such a secret plan against him is that he keeps on bringing fresh witnesses against him and increases his anger toward him (17). The witnesses against Job refer to the afflictions which gave testimony to Job's sinfulness, as thought both Job and his friends. The last line of verse 17, translated literally in KJV and ASV, "Changes and war are with me," refer to this renewal of the witnesses against Job. Job uses the military imagery of fresh troops that an enemy keeps sending. God sends one wave of fresh troops after another, and Job never gets any relief from these invading forces.

The Senselessness of Life (10.18–22)

¹⁸Wherefore then hast thou brought me forth out of the womb?
I had given up the ghost, and no eye had seen me.
¹⁹I should have been as though I had not been;
I should have been carried from the womb to the grave.
²⁰Are not my days few? cease then [Another reading is, *let him cease, and leave me alone*],
And let me alone, that I may take comfort [Heb. *brighten up*] a little,
²¹Before I go whence I shall not return,
Even to the land of darkness and of the shadow of death;
²²The land dark as midnight [Heb. *thick darkness*],
The land of the shadow of death, without any order,
And where the light is as midnight [Heb. *thick darkness*].

Perplexed to despair by failure to understand and by the absurdity that characterizes any purpose he can imagine God entertaining, at the conclusion of this speech Job is right back where he started (ch 3; *cf.* 7.11–16). Job asks why he was ever born in the first place (18f). Better to have died in the womb and never be seen by human eye! (18b). Better to have never existed, simply carried from the womb to the grave! (19). So far as Job can see, his life makes no sense at all.

His speech concludes with one of the most pitiful pleas found in the book (20–22). On the ground that his life will soon be over, Job pleads with God to leave him alone and let him be at peace. Let him get what little comfort he can in the few days he has left before going to the dreary abode of the dead, never to return (20–22).

Job can make no sense at all of his life. Every alternative he can imagine seems absurd. None of them makes any sense. But Job is trying. He is struggling to understand. If he used hard words toward God in chapter 9, in this chapter he is struggling to hold on to his faith. The magnificent struggle continues in the next speech.

Zophar's First Speech (11)

Zophar is the last friend to speak and the hardest on Job. He speaks without the least touch of compassion. But he feels he cannot let Job get away with his protestations of innocence and the complaint against God that went with it. For the first time Job's suffering is directly connected with the sin in his life. The other friends implied as much. But Zophar directly denies Job's claim to be clean in the eyes of God and even asserts that he is not suffering as much as he deserves to suffer.

Zophar's Wish (11.1–6)

Then answered Zophar the Naamathite, and said,
²Should not the multitude of words be answered?
And should a man full of talk be justified?
³Should thy boastings make men hold their peace?
And when thou mockest, shall no man make thee ashamed?
⁴For thou sayest, My doctrine is pure,
And I am clean in thine eyes.
⁵But oh that God would speak,
And open his lips against thee,
⁶And that he would show thee the secrets of wisdom!
For he is manifold in understanding.
Know therefore that God exacteth of thee less than thine iniquity deserveth
    [Or, remitteth (Heb. *causeth to be forgotten*) unto thee of thine iniquity].

1. Reason for Speaking (2–4). Zophar begins by explaining why he must speak. He simply cannot let "the multitude of words" go unanswered (2a). He calls Job, literally, "a man of lips" (2b), as we might say someone is "all talk": "Should a man of lips be justified?" Job just seems to talk on and on. Should we, on that account, just give up the case and pronounce him to be in the right?

"Thy lies" (KJV) is too strong for the term used in verse 3a for Job's claims. The word refers to "empty, idle talk ...especially with the collateral idea of imaginary pretensions or claims" (BDB 95a on No. 907). So Zophar's question is: "Should your boastings (empty claims, pretensions) cause men to hold their peace?" Should such "idle talk" silence us, as if there is anything to it?

The expression used in 3b for Job's speech, "when you mock," is later used by Job to characterize the friends' speeches against him (21.3). But one would have to go back to Job's answer to Eliphaz to find anything that smacks of mockery against the friends (6.24–27). In the immediately preceding speech, Job spoke with the utmost respect toward Bildad (9.2a). His complaint has been against God. So Zophar is probably referring to what he perceives as mockery or scoffing against God. He feels that someone should stand up and put Job to shame for such scoffing.

Verse 4 summarizes what Zophar has in mind when he speaks of Job's "boastings" and mocking. He is talking about Job's protestations of innocence. Job's claim is fairly summarized (*cf.* 9.21; 10.7a and in fact the whole of chapters 9 and 10), though his exact words are not cited.

2. Wish That God Would Speak (5–6). Job wished for a chance to talk with God. He longed for an explanation from God (10.1–2). Zophar wishes that God would speak, and he thinks he knows just what God would say if he did speak. Then the truth would be known—that Job deserves even more affliction than he is getting (6c).

This is certainly the harshest statement made against Job so far. But is Zophar just being mean? I think not. All the friends started with the presumption that suffering always indicates sin in one's life. But Job's complaints and his terrible charges against God have gotten worse, furnishing added evidence of his sin (*cf.* 9.21–24, 28–31; 10.3–7, 13–17). Zophar is not just being mean. He is reacting to Job's complaints and the speculation of chapter 10.

Remember, though, Zophar has no knowledge of sin in Job. He is making an assumption based on Job's afflictions, the evidence of which is reinforced by Job's complaints and charges against God. Zophar feels certain Job has sinned because of his afflictions. He has no other way to explain human suffering than as related to a person's sins. That view leads to great injustice toward Job and also to an attempt to vindicate God that is grounded on error.

"The Secrets of Wisdom" (11.7–12)

⁷Canst thou by searching find out God? [Or, Canst thou find out the deep
  things of God?]
Canst thou find out the Almighty unto perfection?
⁸It is high as heaven [Heb. *The heights of heaven*]; what canst thou do?
Deeper than Sheol; what canst thou know?
⁹The measure thereof is longer than the earth,
And broader than the sea.
¹⁰If he pass through, and shut up,
And call unto judgment [Heb. *call an assembly*], then who can hinder him?
¹¹For he knoweth false men:
He seeth iniquity also, even though he consider it not [Or, and him
  that considereth not].
¹²But vain man is void of understanding,
Yea, man is born *as* a wild ass's colt. [Or, But an empty man will get
  understanding, when a wild ass's colt is born a man.]

Job has been pleading for an explanation of his plight (ch 10). Completely at a loss for understanding, he put forth several speculations with regard to what the explanation might be. Zophar responded with the wish that God would reveal to Job "the secrets of wisdom" (11.6), exposing the reason for Job's suffering. He is confident that, were God to do so, the greatness of Job's sins would stand exposed.

With regard to Job's speculations (in ch 10), he asks Job to consider whether he really thinks he can probe the depths of God's wisdom (7–9). God is much more than a man can comprehend.

As in verse 6, so in verses 10–11, the vastness of God's wisdom and knowledge is applied to human behavior. If he comes along, locks someone up in prison and calls an assembly (ASV margin, NASB), a court (NIV) to render judgment, who can restrain (NKJV margin) or oppose (NIV) him? (10).

But the reason no one can restrain or oppose him (11) is not traced to his superior power but to his knowledge of human conduct: "He knows vain (empty, worthless) men" and sees their evil doing. The last clause is usually handled in one of two ways. Almost all the versions make a question of it: "And shall he not consider (or give attention)?" Shall he look on these things and just let it go without doing anything about it? But the ICC defends another view the NASB also adopts: "He sees iniquity without considering." In this case the clause can be explained from Elihu's assertion in 34.23. God's omniscience gives him complete knowledge of human conduct, so that he does not need to investigate the case further.

On the other hand, one might as well expect a wild donkey to give birth to a man as an empty-headed man to become wise? (12; NKJV; RSV; NASB; NIV).

So the thought is that sins are the reason for calamity, though they may be known only to God, and man may be too dull to understand. Zophar does not place Job, with his complaints and speculations (chs 9–10), in very noble company. No wonder Job begins as he does (in 12.2).

Exhortation to Job: Call to Repentance and Assurance of Consequences to Follow (11.13–20)

¹³If thou set thy heart aright,
And stretch out thy hands toward him;
¹⁴If iniquity be in thy hand, put it far away,
And let not unrighteousness dwell in thy tents.
¹⁵Surely then shalt thou lift up thy face without spot;
Yea, thou shalt be stedfast, and shalt not fear:
¹⁶For thou shalt forget thy misery;
Thou shalt remember it as waters that are passed away,
¹⁷And *thy* life shall be clearer than [Or, arise above] the noonday;
Though there be darkness, it shall be as the morning.
¹⁸And thou shalt be secure, because there is hope;
Yea, thou shalt search *about thee*, and shalt take thy rest in safety.
¹⁹Also thou shalt lie down, and none shall make thee afraid;
Yea, many shall make suit unto thee.
²⁰But the eyes of the wicked shall fail,
And they shall have no way to flee [Heb. *refuge is perished from them*];
And their hope shall be the giving up of the ghost.

Nothing new here! "Zophar's remedy is simple: the usual string of pious advice" (Anderson). Compare Eliphaz (5.8–27). If only Job will put away sin and reach out to God, he will quickly recover and return to a prosperous and secure life (13–19). The present misery will be forgotten, remembered only as so much water under the bridge (16). Life will be bright as the noonday, and even what darkness may come will be as the morning (17). "Yea, many would court your favor" (19b, AB and NKJV; similarly NASB and NIV). "Verse 19b indicates that people will flock to such a man whose prosperity is proof of his friendship with God, either for alms (Pr. 19.6) or for intercessory prayers." So Anderson, who notices the irony that in the end the friends must come to Job for such a favor (42.8).

The wicked, of course, face quite different prospects (20). Their eyes shall fail; escape will be cut off; their only hope is death—the only prospect Job feels he can entertain (10.20–22).

Job's Reply to Zophar (12–14)

As in previous speeches Job responds to the friends (12.2–13.19), then takes his complaint to God (13.20–14.22).

Part One: Address to the Friends (12.1–13.19)

Resentment of the Endeavor to Teach Him Such Fundamental Truth About God (12.1–6)

Then Job answered and said,
²No doubt but ye are the people,
And wisdom shall die with you.
³But I have understanding as well as you;
I am not inferior to you:
Yea, who knoweth not such things as these?
⁴I am as one that is a laughing-stock to his neighbor,
I who called upon God, and he answered:
The just, the perfect man is a laughing-stock.
⁵In the thought of him that is at ease there is contempt for misfortune;
It is ready for them whose foot slippeth.
⁶The tents of robbers prosper,
And they that provoke God are secure;
Into whose hand God bringeth *abundantly.* **[Or, That bring their god in**
  their hand.]

The sarcasm of verse 2 reveals Job's bitter resentment: "No doubt you are the people," meaning the entire human race, "and wisdom will die with you." When you die the last shred of wisdom will have vanished from the earth. What brings this on? I think Job bitterly resents the implication that he is an emptyheaded man with no more understanding than a donkey (11.12). Job replies with bitter sarcasm: "No doubt you are the people," *i.e.* the whole of the people; all others are just dumb brutes, to be compared to a donkey's colt.

The friends are posing as men of wisdom, but Job replies that he is not inferior to them in understanding (3ab). The fact is, he continues, they are only setting forth universally known commonplaces (3c), from which, however, they are drawing erroneous conclusions about Job. Job feels that he has become a laughingstock, a joke (4, NASB), using a word formed from a Hebrew verb meaning to laugh. He has lived with exceptional piety, but look now at what has come of it! What a joke! The absurdity is compounded by having the friends lecture him as they might a child, dealing out to a man of mature piety such elementary instruction on the right relationship with God.

"But such is the treatment which those who fall into misfortune, even though they be righteous men, receive at the hands of those that are at ease and prosperous" (Davidson on 5). NASB margin supplies a literal translation of 5a: "Contempt for calamity is the thought of him who is at ease," who treats misfortune as something "prepared for those whose feet slip." But, in the meantime, the wicked prosper and are secure, God himself bringing prosperity into their hand (6). This view of 6c best suits the following context. It simply repeats the point Job raised in 9.24.

No Special Insight in the Friends (12.7–12)

**⁷But ask now the beasts, and they shall teach thee;
And the birds of the heavens, and they shall tell thee:
⁸Or speak to the earth, and it shall teach thee;
And the fishes of the sea shall declare unto thee.
⁹Who knoweth not in [Or, by] all these,
That the hand of Jehovah hath wrought this,
¹⁰In whose hand is the soul of every living thing,
And the breath [Or, spirit] of all mankind?
¹¹Doth not the ear try words,
Even as the palate tasteth its food?
¹²With aged men is wisdom [Or, With aged men, *ye say*, is wisdom],
And in length of days understanding.**

Zophar spoke of "the secrets of wisdom" (11.6), as if the friends had some insight into these secrets. In fact he summarized what he was confident a revelation of "the secrets of wisdom" would disclose (11.6c). But Job ridiculed their claim to wisdom (12.2) and contended that the views set forth with regard to God's treatment of the righteous (11.13–19) and the wicked (11.20) are not only well understood by himself but, in fact, are commonplaces, universally understood (12.3). The argument continues in verses 7–12 along the same lines.

The matters of observation about the providence of God in human affairs, and especially what Job said about God being ultimately behind the prosperity and security of robbers (6), does not require uncommon knowledge. This lesson can be learned from the creation. The animals, the birds, the earth, and the fish all teach lessons about God (7–8). Consult the beasts, the birds, *etc.* They will teach you.

But what do they teach? That all creation is the work of God (9); that all life, whether that of the lower animals or that of mankind is ultimately dependent upon God (10). This passage then provides support for Job's assertion about God being ultimately behind the prosperity and security of the wicked (6). All life is dependent upon God.

But how are verses 11 and 12 connected with this train of thought? Perhaps they reinforce the idea that the lessons of the creation are not all that hard to learn. The ear puts teaching to the test, just as the palate tastes food (11). Men who have made use of such faculties can be expected to have wisdom and understanding in old age (12).

God's Wisdom and Might (12.13–25)

¹³With God [Heb. *him*] is wisdom and might;
He hath counsel and understanding.
¹⁴Behold, he breaketh down, and it cannot be built again;
He shutteth up a man, and there can be no opening.
¹⁵Behold, he withholdeth the waters, and they dry up;
Again, he sendeth them out, and they overturn the earth.
¹⁶With him is strength and wisdom;
The deceived and the deceiver are his.
¹⁷He leadeth counsellors away stripped,
And judges maketh he fools.
¹⁸He looseth the bond of kings,
And he bindeth their loins with a girdle.
¹⁹He leadeth priests away stripped,
And overthroweth the mighty.
²⁰He removeth the speech of the trusty,

And taketh away the understanding of the elders.
²¹He poureth contempt upon princes,
And looseth the belt of the strong.
²²He uncovereth deep things out of darkness,
And bringeth out to light the shadow of death.
²³He increaseth the nations, and he destroyeth them:
He enlargeth the nations, and he leadeth them captive.
²⁴He taketh away understanding from the chiefs of the people of the earth
    [Or, land],
And causeth them to wander in a wilderness where there is no way.
²⁵They grope in the dark without light;
And he maketh them to stagger [Heb. *wander*] like a drunken man.

Job launches forth into a speech about God that resembles those of the friends. The context of this exposition of God's mighty works is established by the introductory statement (12.2–3) and the conclusion reached (in 13.1–3). He is demonstrating that he knows quite as much as his friends with regard to God's wisdom and power in their various operations. The emphasis throughout is on God's overruling sovereignty and control, even over the high and mighty of the earth.

The Friends' Speeches About God Not to the Point (13.1–3)

Lo, mine eye hath seen all *this,*
Mine ear hath heard and understood it.
²What ye know, *the same* do I know also:
I am not inferior unto you.
³Surely I would speak to the Almighty,
And I desire to reason with God.

Now we see what Job has been up to in the preceding passage. The friends were treating Job as someone who needs to be taught fundamental truth about God and his works. Now he has demonstrated that he is quite as knowledgeable as they and can make their speeches as well as they.

At verse 3 Job returns to the problem first brought to the surface in chapter 9. (See especially 9.2.) The discourses of the friends on the wisdom and power of God have not been to the point. They do not explain Job's calamities. They do not touch top, side nor bottom of the problem of divine providence arising from the prosperity and security of the wicked, which could not occur without God's consent (12.6 and the following verses), while a good man like Job experiences the calamity that is expected to befall very wicked men. Job wants to take his case to God. He will return to this point after his rebuke of the friends in verses 4–12.

Criticism of the Friends (13.4–12)

⁴But ye are forgers of lies;
Ye are all physicians of no value.
⁵Oh that ye would altogether hold your peace!
And it would be your wisdom.
⁶Hear now my reasoning,
And hearken to the pleadings of my lips.
⁷Will ye speak unrighteously for God,
And talk deceitfully for him?
⁸Will ye show partiality to him?
Will ye contend for God?
⁹Is it good that he should search you out?
Or as one deceiveth [Or, mocketh] a man, will ye deceive [Or, mock] him?
¹⁰He will surely reprove you
If ye do secretly show partiality.
¹¹Shall not his majesty make you afraid,
And his dread fall upon you?
¹²Your memorable sayings are proverbs of ashes,
Your defences are defences of clay.

1. *Uselessness of their Counsel (4–6).* Job desired to reason with God (3) having lost all hope of getting any satisfaction from his friends. You are smearing me with lies (4a), says Job. He calls them "worthless physicians" or "physicians of no value"— "quack healers" (AB). In fact, the friends generally speak the truth, as Job acknowledges (9.2a; 12.3; 13.2). But the application to Job is false; it involves a twisting of the truth into a lie. They do not acknowledge that a great deal that is seen in the world cannot be explained consistently with their simplistic teaching about God, his wisdom, power and justice, and the blessing he brings upon the righteous and the judgment upon the wicked. Misapplying the truth of God's wisdom, power and justice, assuming Job's guilt and counselling him to repent in order to be restored, they are like quacks prescribing bandaids and aspirin for a serious illness—or, in Job's case, a condition that they do not know how to diagnose. Job thinks it would be wisdom on their part just to

remain completely silent (5). He calls upon them to listen to the case he wants to make before God (6).

2. The Charge of Partiality (7–11). Job accuses the friends of partiality with regard to the controversy between him and God. Job's complaint is that God seems to be treating him as a sinner, though he is innocent. Without any evidence of Job's guilt, the friends take God's part. Job warns them that God will not stand for it. He will punish partiality, even when that partiality is shown toward himself.

This passage is extremely important as we attempt to define Job's "patience" (Jas 5.11) and to trace the development of Job's faith. He has made terrible charges against God, but his patience lies in the stubborn refusal to abandon God, even under such great trial and in spite of so much misunderstanding. This passage is an example. He manifests faith in God's essential righteousness, confident that God will reprove partiality even when it is shown toward himself.

3. Defenses of Clay (12). The "remembrances" (KJV) of the friends refers to their "memorable sayings" (ASV, NASB), which better preserves the sense of the original than "platitudes" (NKJV) or "maxims" (RSV, NIV). Job calls their "memorable sayings" (*cf.* 4.7; ch 8) "proverbs of ashes," just as useless.

The later versions are certainly correct to substitute "defenses" for the KJV's "bodies" in 12b. The "defenses" of the friends are the reasoned arguments by which they defend their position. Job calls them "defenses of clay"—*i.e.*, as fragile as a shield or bulwark made of clay, crumbling at the first blow.

The Determination to Argue his Case Before God (13.13–19)

¹³Hold your peace, let me alone, that I may speak;
And let come on me what will.
¹⁴Wherefore should I take my flesh in my teeth [Or, At all adventures I will take *etc.*],
And put my life in my hand?
¹⁵Behold, he will slay me; I have no hope [Or, Though he slay me, yet will I wait for him]:
Nevertheless I will maintain [Heb. *argue*] my ways before him.
¹⁶This also shall be my salvation,
That a godless man shall not come before him.
¹⁷Hear diligently my speech,
And let my declaration be in your ears.
¹⁸Behold now, I have set my cause in order;

I know that I am righteous [Or, shall be justified].
¹⁹Who is he that will contend with me?
For then would I hold my peace and give up the ghost. [Or, if I hold my peace,
    I shall give up *etc.*]

After the criticism of the friends (4–12) Job returns to the standpoint of verse 3. He expands upon the determination to take his case to God and to defend his cause before the face of God, though he is still addressing the friends (in 13–19). He is determined to argue his cause and prove his innocence, even at the risk of his life (13–15). He is convinced that this will be his salvation (vindication), for a godless man would not dare to do what Job proposes to do, *i.e.* come before God to argue his cause, but would certainly flee the presence of God (16).

Job concludes with a bold challenge (17–19), again calling upon the friends to hear his case (17). He has arranged his case, knowing that he is in the right (18). Who, he asks, will take the other side and prove me to be guilty? (19a). Perhaps he means in 19b that, if he could get his case heard, he would be satisfied to die (*cf.* 13–15).

Clearly Job has no use for his friends at this point. He has lost confidence in them but not in God. His only hope of vindication lies in an appeal to the highest court.

Part Two: Address to God (13.20–14.22)

Job's Plea to God (13.20–28)

²⁰Only do not two things unto me;
Then will I not hide myself from thy face:
²¹Withdraw thy hand far from me;
And let not thy terror make me afraid.
²²Then call thou, and I will answer;
Or let me speak, and answer thou me.
²³How many are mine iniquities and sins?
Make me to know my transgression and my sin.
²⁴Wherefore hidest thou thy face,
And holdest me for thine enemy?
²⁵Wilt thou harass a driven leaf?
And wilt thou pursue the dry stubble?
²⁶For thou writest bitter things against me,
And makest me to inherit the iniquities of my youth:
²⁷Thou puttest my feet also in the stocks,

And markest all my paths;
Thou settest a bound to the soles of my feet:
²⁸Though I am like [Heb. *And he is like*] a rotten thing that consumeth,
Like a garment that is moth-eaten.

Job's speech continues, but now, instead of specially addressing the friends, he turns to God.

Job is confident that he would be able to make out his case if only God would not terrify him with his power (20f). Thus he renews the plea of 9.34f. He would be willing to act as either plaintiff or defendant in the legal controversy (22).

Job wants to "speak to the Almighty" and "reason with God" (3, *cf.* 13). But what would he say? Verses 23–25 contain questions Job would present for God's answer if given the opportunity. They indicate the things he wants to know. He wants to know the sins for which he is being afflicted (23) and the reason God is treating him as an enemy (24). Further, would God harrass one already so helpless? (25). He was like a powerful wind bringing all its force to bear on "a driven leaf" or "the dry stubble."

The section closes with a complaint (26–28). God is like a judge writing a condemnatory sentence against Job (26; *cf.* Isa 10.1), making him pay for the sins of his youth, so long past, dealt with and forgotten. In verse 27 "Job compares himself to a malefactor, at one time (a) held fast in the stocks, at another (b) narrowly watched, and (c) unable to pass beyond prescribed bounds" (Driver in ICC, I, 126). The figures "all have to do with circumscribing the movements of a man" (Rowley). Finally, in a transition to the next passage Job speaks of himself in the third person as one member of the human race (28). God has treated him as described (in 26f), though he was already as far gone as some rotten thing or a moth-eaten garment.

Plea Based on the Sad Condition of Man's Life on Earth (14.1–6)

Man, that is born of a woman,
Is of few days, and full of trouble.
²He cometh forth like a flower, and is cut down [Or, withereth]:
He fleeth also as a shadow, and continueth not.
³And dost thou open thine eyes upon such a one,
And bringest me into judgment with thee?
⁴Who can bring a clean thing out of an unclean? not one. [Or, Oh, that a
      clean thing could come out of an unclean? not one can.]
⁵Seeing his days are determined,

The number of his months is with thee,
And thou hast appointed his bounds that he cannot pass;
⁶Look away from him, that he may rest [Heb. *cease*],
Till he shall accomplish [Or, *have pleasure in*], as a hireling, his day.

Job extends his view to consider the general condition of mankind. Life at best is short and full of trouble (1–2). On top of that, though man appears to be unworthy of notice, yet God watches him closely and brings him into judgment (3).

Perhaps judgment (in 3) is thought of as a process of purification like a refiner's fire, as in Malachi 4.1–6, in which God is using the purifying fire of judgment to produce some clean thing. But is he not expecting the impossible, that a clean thing should be brought forth from an unclean? Look at the history of the human race. How is it possible to bring forth something clean out of all that uncleanness? "That which is born of the flesh is flesh" (John 3.6), and man cannot be more than he is (4).

Since mankind's life is so limited (5), Job sends up the pitiful plea that God would not give him so much attention (*cf.* 3), but instead give him a break and let him just get what little pleasure he can out of life (6). At this point Job is not making an argument about what is just for man but begging, making a pitful plea, not only for himself but for all men whose lives must be lived amidst such hardness and sadness.

Job's Pathetic Plea Strengthened by Reference to the Sad Destiny of Mankind (14.7–12)

⁷For there is hope of a tree,
If it be cut down, that it will sprout again,
And that the tender branch thereof will not cease.
⁸Though the root thereof wax old in the earth,
And the stock thereof die in the ground;
⁹Yet through the scent of water it will bud,
And put forth boughs like a plant.
¹⁰But man dieth, and is laid low:
Yea, man giveth up the ghost, and where is he?
¹¹*As* the waters fail from the sea,
And the river wasteth and drieth up;
¹²So man lieth down and riseth not:
Till the heavens be no more, they shall not awake,
Nor be roused out of their sleep.

Job's description of man's brief, hard life has led to the plea that God might leave him alone and let him just finish out "his day" (6). His plea is now strengthened by reference to the hopelessness of his condition after death. He just dies, and that is all there is to him. All the more reason to take pity on him and, at least, let him salvage what he can out of this brief life.

Mankind does not even have the hope of a tree, Job reasons (7–10). A tree may be cut down only to sprout again. But once man has been laid low and breathes his last breath, what becomes of him? He is not like a tree that may come back to life. He could more suitably be compared to the waters of the sea or of a river, which evaporate never to return (11–12). So with man. At death he lies down never to rise again.

Longing for Life After Death (14.13–17)

¹³Oh that thou wouldest hide me in Sheol,
That thou wouldest keep me secret, until thy wrath be past,
That thou wouldest appoint me a set time, and remember me!
¹⁴If a man die, shall he live *again*?
All the days of my warfare would [Or, will …shall come] I wait,
Till my release [Or, change] should come.
¹⁵Thou wouldest call, and I would answer thee [Or, shalt call and I will *etc.*]:
Thou wouldest have a desire to the work of thy hands.
¹⁶But now thou numberest my steps:
Dost thou not watch over my sin?
¹⁷My transgression is sealed up in a bag,
And thou fastenest up mine iniquity.

Job feels sure the wrath of God would pursue him to the grave. He has no hope of a return to God's favor this side of death. He therefore wishes and prays that God would keep him in Sheol until God's wrath has been satisfied and is past, that God would set a time to remember him (13).

The question of 14a, "If a man die, shall he live?" seems blurted out as an exclamation, as if Job suddenly realizes just what his longing (13) amounted to. It seems incredible that a man might die and yet live. But if only it might be! If only a man might live, having once died (14a)! Job would be willing to wait through all the days of his warfare until his change (or release) should come (14b), when God would remember and call for him, finally having a desire for the man he had created (15; contrast 10.8–17).

But this "change" has not come yet, and Job feels himself under the wrath of God (*cf.* 13b) in the present. His present treatment by God is placed alongside this longing (16–17). Instead of giving a poor man a break and looking away (*cf.* 6), God watches carefully, making sure to notice every sin (16). God saves up Job's sins rather than pardoning (9.21) and removing them "as far as the east is from the west" (Psa 103.12). The speech closes with a hopelessness.

Closing Expression of Hopelessness (14.18–22)

¹⁸But the mountain falling cometh to nought [Heb. *fadeth away*];
And the rock is removed out of its place;
¹⁹The waters wear the stones;
The overflowings thereof wash away the dust of the earth:
So thou destroyest the hope of man.
²⁰Thou prevailest for ever against him, and he passeth;
Thou changest his countenance, and sendest him away.
²¹His sons come to honor, and he knoweth it not;
And they are brought low, but he perceiveth it not of them.
²²But his flesh upon him hath pain,
And his soul within him mourneth. [Or, Only for himself his flesh hath pain, and for himself his soul mourneth.]

God's present treatment of Job (16–17), so contrary to Job's longing (13–17), leads to the concluding despair. The destruction of man's hope is compared to powerful natural forces eroding away mountain, rocks and dust (18–19). With such severe treatment as man is accorded by God, he is surely doomed to perish (20–22). Once he is gone, he will know nothing of the fortunes or misfortunes of his sons (21). He will know only the misery of his own condition (22).

Again and again we will see conflicting feelings and expressions in Job. On the one hand, the expressions of frustration and despair, and perhaps even more, the complaints against God and the conviction that he is being unjustly treated by God reveal the reality of the trial that Job is undergoing. His faith will survive the testing, but not without being strained almost to the breaking point. The value of such passages as the concluding words of this speech (14.18–22) is the light they shed on Job's trial. If he simply takes it all without complaint, putting on a happy face and a show of piety, we would never understand the greatness of the trial. We would have no insight into what he is feeling and experiencing spiritually. But Job's honesty and outspokenness reveal in this man the thoughts that prey upon the minds of many of us. They are put out in the open, so that an answer can be given to them and we can gather the food that nourishes our own faith.

On the other hand, we become witnesses to a mighty struggle to hold on to God. Look at the reflections of faith we have already heard from Job. His warning to the friends that God will not put up with partiality or favoritism, even when it is shown toward himself (13.7–11), is a wonderful expression of confidence in God and his justice. So also is the determination to take his case to God (ch 13). Job has lost confidence in his friends and their ability to minister to his need, but he has not lost confidence in God. Finally, the hopelessness of 14.7–12 is immediately followed by the wish for a life after death, in which the present state might be reversed. The hopelessness is also followed by an expression of determination, if only such a future life might be, to wait on God however long it takes until the warfare is over (14.13–15; cf. 13.13–19).

Job's faith is not yet at its highest peak. That comes in chapter 19. But it is a beginning. Job is on his way. So the other side of the negative picture, which reveals the severity of the trial, is the mighty struggle for faith and hope. What a glorious battle for faith this man is fighting!

Second Round of Speeches: Continuation of the Discussion (Job 15–21)

After Job's initial complaint in chapter 3, Eliaphaz initiated the debate by cautioning Job about "vexation." Such bitter resentment against divine providence could lead to his destruction, and a man cannot be more righteous than God. Then one after another the friends each made speeches about God. Each dwells upon God, his attributes and man's proper place in relation to him. They assured Job of a change of fortune if only he would turn to God and lead the pious life. That is what they thought Job needed to hear.

Their arguments take another turn in the second round of speeches. Two points in the speeches of Job seem to lead them to a change of subject. On the one hand, Job insisted that the friends' speeches were beside the mark, that he did not need to be taught about God. After all their speeches did not reflect extraordinary knowledge, but only commonplace truth that is known by all pious people. In fact, Job demonstrated that he can make the friends' speeches as well as they could, that he knows as much as they do about God.

On the other hand, he complained that he has a problem with God; he feels he has been wronged; he wants to take his case to God. Meantime, wicked people often seem to prosper in spite of their impiety.

As a result, Eliphaz begins to change his view of Job. His initial address took the view that Job is a pious man who is being chastised for sins that are common to man. Now he begins to see Job as a wicked man, his view being proved by Job's own speeches. Arguments and reflection on the character of God have made no impression on Job. The friends now see him as a type of the wicked man and his sufferings as a type of the calamities that befall such a man. They view his rebellious impatience as a typical attitude of the wicked under suffering.

So the subject of the friends' speeches in Round Two is not God, primarily, but man, and especially the wicked man as history and experience show him to be dealt with in the providence of God. These speeches are a warning to Job, aimed at bringing him to repentance. But the actual effect of them is to precipitate a crisis, for the new arguments can be tested by experience, and, by the end of this round of speeches, Job has crushed them.

Eliphaz' Second Speech (15)

Part One: Eliphaz' Condemnation of Job (15.2–16)

This speech marks an advance upon Eliphaz' first address. Remember that he had not assumed great iniquity in Job nor accused him of impiety at first (4.1–11). But Job's words now seem to provide evidence of bad character in Job. So, after Job's first three responses to the friends, Eliphaz asserts: It is not I that condemn you; you stand self-condemned by your own words.

Job Condemned by His Own Speeches (15.1–6)

Then answered Eliphaz the Temanite, and said,
²Should a wise man make answer with vain knowledge [Heb. *knowledge of wind*],
And fill himself with the east wind?
³Should he reason with unprofitable talk,
Or with speeches wherewith he can do no good?
⁴Yea, thou doest away with fear,

And hinderest [Heb. *diminisheth*] devotion [Or, meditation before God.
⁵For thine iniquity teacheth thy mouth [Or, thy mouth teacheth thine iniquity],
And thou choosest the tongue of the crafty.
⁶Thine own mouth condemneth thee, and not I;
Yea, thine own lips testify against thee.

Eliphaz charges that Job's speeches are not those of a wise man, but are rather evidence of iniquity in Job.

Job claimed wisdom equal to that of his friends (12.2f) and demonstrated it with his own presentation on the subject of God's wisdom and might (12.13–25), asserting in conclusion that he knows as much as the friends about the matters on which they are instructing him, no doubt feeling that he had proved his point (13.1–2). Dismissing the friends as useless, he expressed the wish to take his case to God (13.3–12).

Eliphaz begins by asking Job whether his speeches are those of a wise man. To Eliphaz they show Job to be a man full of hot air, a windbag (2). His speeches can do no good (3), but in fact stand to do harm, doing away with fear of God among men and reducing devotion to God (4). He no doubt refers to Job's assertions about the moral indifference of God's rule (9.21–24) and the fact that a pious man suffers so much while the wicked prosper (12.4–6). Such talk, says Eliphaz, will discourage people from serving God. No more proof of Job's iniquity is needed than that which comes from his own mouth (5–6).

The Presumptuous Claim to Superior Knowledge (15.7–16)

⁷Art thou the first man that was born?
Or wast thou brought forth before the hills?
⁸Hast thou heard the secret counsel of God? [Or, Dost thou hearken in
    the council?]
And dost thou limit wisdom to thyself?
⁹What knowest thou, that we know not?
What understandest thou, which is not in us?
¹⁰With us are both the gray-headed and the very aged men,
Much elder than thy father.
¹¹Are the consolations of God too small for thee,
Even the word that is gentle toward thee? [Or, is there any secret thing
    with thee?]
¹²Why doth thy heart carry thee away?
And why do thine eyes flash,

¹³That against God thou turnest thy spirit,
And lettest words go out of thy mouth?
¹⁴What is man, that he should be clean?
And he that is born of a woman, that he should be righteous?
¹⁵Behold, he putteth no trust in his holy ones;
Yea, the heavens are not clean in his sight:
¹⁶How much less one that is [Or, that which is] abominable and corrupt,
A man that drinketh iniquity like water!

When we reach verse 11 we see that Eliphaz has primarily in mind the friends' attempts at consolation. These "consolations of God" most-ly amounted to assurances about the recovery and the prosperity that would surely be Job's once he seeks after God, repenting of any sins he may have. Each of the friends offered the same consolation (*cf.* 5.8–27; 8.5–7; 11.13–20). But Job considered himself, and, in fact, had been, a man "who called upon God" and otherwise lived a pious life. So such consolation is nothing but mockery (17.2; 21.3) and Job himself a "laughingstock" (12.4). Their comfort does not comfort. It is all beside the point. They failed to find an answer to the problem. Job has no an-swer either, but he knows that for all their claims to offering a solution, they failed to diagnose the problem. Perhaps this analysis will help us to see where Eliphaz is coming from when he accuses Job of claiming superior knowledge.

He demands to know the source of such superior wisdom and knowl-edge. Are you the first man to be born? (7). The point is perhaps clarified by questions Jehovah himself asks later about the creation, telling Job in effect: No doubt you know all about these things, since you were already born "and the number of your days is great" (38.4–7, 21). So Eliphaz asks: Were you back there in the beginning, so that you know all about the way the world functions?

Further: Do you have sole access to "the secret counsel of God," so that you have full knowledge of the mysteries of God? (8a). Are you the only one with wisdom? (8b). What do you know and understand that we do not? (9).

Eliphaz is trying to reduce Job's pretensions to an absurdity. No, Job was not there at the beginning. He does not have access to special knowledge. In fact, Eliphaz continues, the aged, all the people that have really lived a long time, who are "older than your father," are on our side of the question (10).

Finally: "Are the consolations of God (communicated through the friends) too small for you…" (11), so that you treat them with contempt, as if they are nothing, and brush them aside so easily and disrespectfully?

Job is accused of irreverence toward God (in 12 and 13). He had reacted to the consolations of God as if they were nothing, and, in fact, the attempt to minister comfort to Job had made him angry. So Eliphaz asks: Why do you permit passion to carry you away into such charges against God, while your eyes flash with anger?

What justifies such passion? Job claims to be innocent (*cf.* 13.15b–19). But who in fact can claim innocence? "What is man, that he should be clean? *etc.*" (14).

Verses 15 and 16 wrap up the whole line of thought beginning at verse 7. No, Job certainly cannot claim special access to "the secret counsel of God" (8). God does not even put confidence in his angels, the holy ones (15), revealing to them the secrets of his purposes (*cf.* 4:18f). How much less would he take into his counsel a man like Job, who spews out in his speeches (*cf.* 4–6) the iniquity he has taken in, gulping it up like water? (16).

Eliphaz does not specifically name Job as the man he has in mind in verse 16. But after verses 5 and 6, and also in light of the comparison with Elihu's use of this imagery (in 34.7–9), surely he has Job specially in mind. Verse 16, therefore, reveals the way Eliphaz has come to see Job. All men are sinners, of course, missing the mark occasionally (14). But Job is not just a sinner in the sense of a godly man who occasionally falls into sin. He is a wicked man, an impious man. His own words prove as much. Such is the position of Eliphaz at this point.

Part Two: The True Doctrine of the Wicked Man (15.17–35)

¹⁷I will show thee, hear thou me;
And that which I have seen I will declare:
¹⁸(Which wise men have told
From their fathers, and have not hid it;
¹⁹Unto whom alone the land was given,
And no stranger passed among them):
²⁰The wicked man travaileth with pain all his days,
Even the number of years that are laid up for the oppressor.
²¹A sound of terrors is in his ears;
In prosperity the destroyer shall come upon him.
²²He believeth not that he shall return out of darkness,
And he is waited for of the sword.
²³He wandereth abroad for bread, *saying*, Where is it?

He knoweth that the day of darkness is ready at his hand.
²⁴Distress and anguish make him afraid;
They prevail against him, as a king ready to the battle.
²⁵Because he hath stretched out his hand against God,
And behaveth himself proudly [Or, biddeth defiances] against the Almighty;
²⁶He runneth upon him with a *stiff* neck,
With [Or, upon] the thick bosses of his bucklers;
²⁷Because he hath covered his face with his fatness,
And gathered fat upon his loins;
²⁸And he hath dwelt in desolate [Or, cut off] cities,
In houses which no man inhabited [Or, would inhabit],
Which were ready to become heaps;
²⁹He shall not be rich, neither shall his substance continue,
Neither shall their possessions be extended on the earth [Or, their produce
bend to the earth].
³⁰He shall not depart out of darkness;
The flame shall dry up his branches,
And by the breath of *God's* [Heb. *his*] mouth shall he go away.
³¹Let him not trust in vanity, deceiving himself;
For vanity shall be his recompense.
³²It shall be accomplished [Or, paid in full] before his time,
And his branch shall not be green.
³³He shall shake off his unripe grape as the vine,
And shall cast off his flower as the olive-tree.
³⁴For the company of the godless shall be barren,
And fire shall consume the tents of bribery.
³⁵They conceive mischief, and bring forth iniquity,
And their heart prepareth deceit.

Eliphaz contended that Job does not speak as a wise man, but rather, his complaints against God about his own mistreatment and the prosperity of the wicked expose the iniquity that is in him (2–6). He argued that Job's contempt for the efforts of the friends to help him reveals a claim to superior insight into the counsel of God, which, however, can not possibly be found in such a man as he (7–16). Now he is ready to proclaim the true doctrine about the wicked man, as opposed to Job's complaints and assertions, which are calculated to diminish piety among men. His explanation about the reason for the wicked man's calamities (25f) is reminiscent of his characterization of Job's opposition to God (12f). Plainly, Eliphaz intends this exposition of the true doctrine of the wicked man as a warning to Job. He says "the wicked man," but he is thinking of Job.

The Sources of His Knowledge (17–19)

As in 4.12–16, Eliphaz begins by describing the source of the doctrine he will put before Job. It derives from his own experience (17), which, however, is no novelty but represents the consistent moral tradition of wise men handed down from their fathers before the advent of contaminating foreign influences (18f).

The Truth About the Wicked Man (20–35)

The main thrust of this passage is not difficult to make out, but it is harder to see upon closer analysis. In general, the terrible life a wicked man should expect is interwoven with descriptions of his character explaining the reason behind his difficulties. *The first verses (20–24) seem to be mostly descriptive of psychological pain—his troubled conscience and presentiments of disaster.*

It seems clear that *verses 25–28 develop the reasons for his troubles—his defiance of God and brutish fleshly life.* Readers of the English versions find the thoughts connected differently in different versions, and I do not have the expertise in Hebrew that would equip me to choose between them. But looking at the content of the verses, perhaps the following analysis of the connections of thought is reasonable. After the military imagery is introduced in verse 24—distress and anxiety prevailing against Job as might a king with his armies well prepared for battle— Eliphaz continues: Because Job challenged the Almighty (as described in 25), God comes down upon him like a warrior in his armor (26). Because he indulged himself so lavishly, thus covering his body with fat (27), he is reduced to dwelling in desolate cities and houses not fit for human habitation (28).

Finally, verses 29–35 depict the hopelessness of this man's life. He will not possess enduring wealth (29) nor be able to escape from darkness (30). Any hope he might entertain is vanity (or emptiness), which will be his reward (31). His trouble will come "before his time" (32) like a vine dropping off its unripe grapes or the olive tree casting off its flower (33). For the company of the godless cannot escape disaster, despite all their wicked scheming (34–35).

Let Job take warning. This is his destiny if he does not repent of his wicked complaints against God. That is Eliphaz' message.

Job's Reply to Eliphaz (16–17)

Job does not directly answer Eliphaz' speech about the wicked man. He will later. But for now he summarily dismisses Eliphaz along with the others (16.1–5), then renews his complaint (16.6–17).

Brief and Contemptuous Dismissal of His "Comforters" (16.1–5)

Then Job answered and said,
²I have heard many such things:
Miserable [Or, Wearisome] comforters are ye all.
³Shall vain words [Heb. *words of wind*] have an end?
Or what provoketh thee that thou answerest?
⁴I also could speak as ye do;
If your soul were in my soul's stead,
I could join words together against you,
And shake my head at you.
⁵*But* I would strengthen you with my mouth,
And the solace of my lips would assuage *your grief.*

Job has had his fill of such pious platitudes. He has had about all the "comfort" he can stand. *Miserable comforters* (2) is literally *comforters of trouble.* The Hebrew word is the same as "mischief" or "trouble" at the end of Eliphaz' speech (15.35), the word being flung back at the friends. Far from communicating "the comforts of God" (15.11), their "comfort" (*cf.* 2.11) is no comfort at all, but only increases his trouble. Will there be no end of such "words of wind" (literal translation)? (3a). Job cannot imagine what provoked them to answer instead of simply dropping the controversy as he wished (3b). Recall his wish that they would simply keep silent and let that be their wisdom (13.5).

Such talk requires no great skill. "I also could speak as you do," says Job, if our positions were reversed (4). But instead, he would be a true comforter to them (5).

Complaint of God's Treatment of Him, Despite His Innocence (16.6–17)

⁶Though I speak, my grief is not assuaged;
And though I forbear, what am I eased [Heb. *what departeth from me*]?
⁷But now he hath made me weary:
Thou hast made desolate all my company.
⁸And thou hast laid fast hold on me [Or, shrivelled me up], *which* is a witness
   against me:

And my leanness riseth up against me,
It testifieth to my face.
⁹He hath torn me in his wrath, and persecuted [Or, hated] me;
He hath gnashed upon me with his teeth:
Mine adversary sharpeneth his eyes upon me.
¹⁰They have gaped upon me with their mouth;
They have smitten me upon the cheek reproachfully:
They gather themselves together against me.
¹¹God delivereth me to the ungodly,
And casteth me into the hands of the wicked.
¹²I was at ease, and he brake me asunder;
Yea, he hath taken me by the neck, and dashed me to pieces:
He hath also set me up for his mark.
¹³His archers [Or, arrows; Or, mighty ones] compass me round about;
He cleaveth my reins asunder, and doth not spare;
He poureth out my gall upon the ground.
¹⁴He breaketh me with breach upon breach;
He runneth upon me like a giant [Or, mighty man].
¹⁵I have sewed sackcloth upon my skin,
And have laid [Or, defiled] my horn in the dust.
¹⁶My face is red with weeping,
And on my eyelids is the shadow of death;
¹⁷Although there is no violence in my hands,
And my prayer is pure.

No longer directly addressing the friends, in this section Job sometimes speaks directly to God (7b, 8) and sometimes speaks about him in the third person—a kind of soliloquy. The friends have criticized Job's speeches. But Job complains that nothing relieves his misery—neither speaking nor forbearing (6). God has worn him out, Job complains, and then further blames God for isolating him from his friends (7). The next verse explains how: The affliction brought on him by God is a witness, testifying to his sinfulness (8; cf. 10.17). Like a beast of prey, God has attacked him (9ab), and that has been followed by hostility from men (9c–11).

God's sudden attack upon him is further described in verses 12–14. Job compares himself to a target for God's arrows, piercing to his vital parts (12f) and then a fort broken by repeated breaches and stormed by a warrior (14).

The description of the miserable condition to which Job had been reduced by these hostile attacks follows in verses 15f—all despite his innocence (17). *My prayer is pure*, he protests. He does not have violence in his hands such as would explain why prayers are not answered (*cf.* Isa 1.15). His hands are holy as he lifts them up to God (*cf.* 1 Tim 2.8). Yet this man who had once "called upon God and he answered" (12.4), now can get no response.

Cry for Ultimate Vindication (16.18–17.9)

¹⁸O earth, cover not thou my blood,
And let my cry have no *resting* -place [Or, have no more place].
¹⁹Even now, behold, my witness is in heaven,
And he that voucheth for me is on high.
²⁰My friends scoff at me:
But mine eye poureth out tears unto God,
²¹That he would maintain the right of a man with God [Or, That one might
    plead for a man with God, as a son of man *pleadeth* for his neighbor],
And of a son of man with his neighbor!
²²For when a few years are come,
I shall go the way whence I shall not return.
My spirit is consumed, my days are extinct,
The grave is *ready* for me.
²Surely there are mockers [Heb. *mockery*] with me,
And mine eye dwelleth upon their provocation.
³Give now a pledge, be surety for me with thyself;
Who is there that will strike hands with me?
⁴For thou hast hid their heart from understanding:
Therefore shalt thou not exalt *them*.
⁵He that denounceth his friends for a prey [Heb. *portion*],
Even the eyes of his children shall fail.
⁶But he hath made me a byword of the people;
And they spit in my face.
⁷Mine eye also is dim by reason of sorrow,
And all my members are as a shadow.
⁸Upright men shall be astonished at this,
And the innocent shall stir up himself against the godless.
⁹Yet shall the righteous hold on his way,
And he that hath clean hands shall wax stronger and stronger.

The thought of his innocence (16.17) is Job's breaking point, and leads to the outburst found here. He claims to be innocent but appears to be guilty. In the first place, the afflictions brought on him by Jehovah are witnesses against him (10.17; 16.8), creating a presumption of guilt. On that basis his friends assume his guilt, and his complaints against God transformed the presumption of guilt into a certainty in their minds (15.2–6). Though Job's prayer is pure and not stained by guilt (16.17), yet he can get no response from God as in time past (12.4). So he fully expects to die a martyr's death, with the appearance of guilt upon him. That is the thought he cannot endure—to be thought guilty and with even his protestations silenced. So he begs God to vindicate him, even after death, and pleads for a pledge that God will eventually establish his innocence.

1. *The Cry for Vindication (16.18)*. The section begins with an outburst, which is addressed neither to the friends nor to God, but to the earth. It is a plea that his innocent blood not be covered, but permitted to cry out for things to be set right (16.18 *cf.* Gen 4.10; Isa 26.21; Ezek 24.7f). Job cannot endure the prospect of continuing to be thought guilty, even after death, and he with no voice to protest.

2. *A Witness in Heaven (16.19–21)*. Job wishes that his blood might cry out until justice is done. But might not his blood cry out throughout all eternity without ever being heard, without ever anyone coming forward with the evidence that will set matters right? Job is confident that he has a witness in heaven, who can stand up and vouch for him (19). Job expects nothing from his friends, who only scoff at his protestations of innocence, but lifts up his tearful plea to God that he would take up his case and vindicate him or, perhaps, that there might be someone to plead his case with God (20f).

The witness Job has in mind is most likely God himself—the one to whom blood cries from the ground (*cf.* Gen 4.10); the one known to be in heaven or on high (Job 31.2); a witness to human affairs (Gen 31.50; Jer 29.23; 42.5); the one to whom Job has consistently appealed, including the present context (16.20f; 17.3f). Job considers God to be the one who has provided the evidence against him (8). Yet he has no other to whom he can turn for justice. In effect, it is a plea to God against God. He accuses God of mistreating him. But it is only God whom he can trust to establish his innocence. What a magnificent struggle to hold on to God!

3. *No Hope in This Life (16.22–17.2)*. Job explains the reason for such a hope. He is convinced that he faces death without hope of restoration in this life. The false hopes held out by the friends on condition of repentance is nothing more than "mockery," a provocation. So his plea must be to God for vindication (*i.e.*, for things to be made right) after death.

4. Plea for a Pledge (17.3). Job therefore begs God for a pledge that his innocence would ultimately be established (3). The Hebrew for giving a pledge or giving surety for one (S. 6148) has the idea of guaranteeing that something will be done, as, for example, giving assurance that a debt will be paid (*cf.* Prov 11.15; 20.16; 27.13), perhaps pledging property to secure a debt (Neh 5.3). (See BDB, 786b and Ges. 650f.) Striking hands is a gesture that seals the pledge or suretyship. Compare Proverbs 6.1 and 17.18 where it is also parallel to becoming surety. Compare our "shaking hands on the deal."

5. Grounds of Job's Plea (17.4–5). These verses supply grounds for Job's plea to God and are connected with 3b as follows: If God does not "strike hands" with Job, then no one will. God is his only hope. His friends have no understanding of his case and certainly will not be permitted to triumph in the controversy (4). Job hen characterizes the cruelty of his friends in a line that seems proverbial (5), comparing them to someone that betrays his friends for gain (*cf.* 6.27 and perhaps 13.7–11).

6. Effects of God's Hard Treatment of Job (17.6–9). Verses 6f return to the "description of God's hard treatment of Job" (ICC). "This thought of the perverse obstinacy and cruelty of his friends leads Job again to a gloomy survey of his whole condition (*cf.* 16.22–17.2)," concluding with the effect of such sufferings of the godly on the minds of upright men (6–9, Davidson). They are astonished at what they see in Job and "their moral indignation" is aroused against godless men who prosper (8). In spite of all, however, the righteous will hold to their course and emerge victorious (9)—this, perhaps, in contrast to Eliphaz' charge (15.4). Job is really expressing "his own sentiments and resolution" (Davidson). His confidence in his way of life as the right way to live has not been shaken in spite of his trials (*cf.* 1.9–11; 2.4f). He may not understand the ways of God, but his moral integrity remains intact.

Final Repudiation of the False Hopes Held Out by the Friends (17.10–16)

¹⁰But as for you all, come on now again;
And I shall not find [Or, For I find not] a wise man among you.
¹¹My days are past, my purposes are broken off,
Even the thoughts [Or, possessions] of my heart.
¹²They change the night into day:
The light, *say they,* is near unto [Or, because of] the darkness.

¹³If I look [Or, hope, Sheol is my house; I have spread …I have said …and
where now is my hope?] for Sheol as my house;
If I have spread my couch in the darkness;
¹⁴If I have said to corruption [Or, the pit], Thou art my father;
To the worm, *Thou art* my mother, and my sister;
¹⁵Where then is my hope?
And as for my hope, who shall see it?
¹⁶It shall go down to the bars of Sheol,
When once there is rest in the dust.

Recall the prospects of recovery the friends have continually put before Job on condition of repentance. In effect Job challenges them to bring on their stupid arguments, confident that he would not find a wise man among them (10). Job is convinced that he has no more hope in this life (11).

Verse 12 is obscure but seems to allude to the bright prospects the friends hold out to Job if only he will turn to God. *They change the night to day: The light is near unto the darkness.* Just seek God, they tell Job, and recovery and prosperity will soon follow.

But the truth is, the only hope that remains for Job is in the grave (13–16). If he looks for Sheol as his home (13) and the corruption (or the pit) and maggot of the grave are greeted as his family members (14), where is his hope? (15). Only in the gloom of Sheol, once he has been laid to rest in the dust (16).

Final Reflection

So Job again concludes with an expression of hopelessness. But despite the gloomy conclusion, Job is struggling mightily to hold on to God. After the complete despair of his first speeches (chs 3, 6–7, 9–10) Job had begun to make steady progress. He had risen to the confidence expressed in chapter 13 that he would be able to establish his cause if only he had the opportunity to reason with God. That was followed by the wish that there might be a life after death (14.7–15) and now the plea for vindication after death (16.8–17.9). Job has lost all confidence in his friends, but he cannot give God up. God is all he has. As readers, we are permitted to observe a mighty struggle for faith. But it is not over, and the level of Job's faith will rise yet higher in his next speech.

Bildad's Second Speech:
Accusing Job of Overturning the Moral Order of the World in Order to Justify Himself (18)

After a brief rebuke directed at Job (2–4) Bildad comes to the main theme of his speech, in which he reinforces and expands upon the thesis of Eliphaz (5–21).

Response to Job Introducing the Main Theme of the Speech (18.2–4)

Then answered Bildad the Shuhite, and said,
How long will ye hunt for words?
Consider, and afterwards we will speak.
³Wherefore are we counted as beasts,
***And* are become unclean in your sight?**
⁴Thou that tearest thyself in thine anger,
Shall the earth be forsaken for thee?
Or shall the rock be removed out of its place?

Bildad has no patience with Job. As he sees it, Job is not paying attention to the message of the friends, but instead, endlessly searching for words to answer the friends and to justify himself. He calls upon Job to pay serious attention to their argument, "and then we can speak" (2). Argument would be useless otherwise.

We must recall the opinions Job expressed of his friends and their speeches in order to understand Bildad's question in verse 3. Job considered that God "hid their heart from understanding" (17.4a). They might go on with their arguments, but Job did not expect to find a wise man among them (17.10). What are they, then? Nothing but stupid animals? Bildad deeply resents being regarded as no more than stupid cattle (3).

Perhaps with reference to Job's complaint that God had torn him in his wrath (16.10), Bildad describes Job as tearing himself in his anger (4a). The questions in 4bc speak to Job's protestations of innocence, complaints of unjust treatment, and his longing for vindication, if not now, then after death. The questions are tantamount to asking: Shall the established moral order of the world be set aside or rearranged so that you can be justified? This established moral order is then set forth in the remainder of the chapter.

Destiny of the Wicked According to the Moral Order (cf. 4bc) of the World (18.5–21)

⁵Yea, the light of the wicked shall be put out,
And the spark [Or, flame] of his fire shall not shine.
⁶The light shall be dark in his tent,
And his lamp above [Or, beside] him shall be put out.
⁷The steps of his strength shall be straitened,
And his own counsel shall cast him down.
⁸For he is cast into a net by his own feet,
And he walketh upon the toils.
⁹A gin shall take *him* by the heel,
And a snare shall lay hold on him.
¹⁰A noose is hid for him in the ground,
And a trap for him in the way.
¹¹Terrors shall make him afraid on every side,
And shall chase him at his heels.
¹²His strength shall be hunger-bitten,
And calamity shall be ready at his side [Or, for his halting].
¹³The members of his body [Heb. *bars of his skin*] shall be devoured,
Yea, the first-born of death shall devour his members.
¹⁴He shall be rooted out of his tent where he trusteth;
And he shall be brought [Heb. *it shall* (or, *thou shalt*) *bring him*] to the king
    of terrors.
¹⁵There shall dwell in his tent that which is none of his [Or, It shall dwell in his
    tent, that it be no more his; or, because it is none of his]:
Brimstone shall be scattered upon his habitation.
¹⁶His roots shall be dried up beneath,
And above shall his branch be cut off [Or, wither].
¹⁷His remembrance shall perish from the earth,
And he shall have no name in the street.
¹⁸He shall be driven from light into darkness,
And chased out of the world.
¹⁹He shall have neither son nor son's son among his people,
Nor any remaining where he sojourned.
²⁰They that come after shall be astonished at his day,
As they that went before were affrighted [Heb. *laid hold on horror*]. [Or, They
    that dwell in the west are ...as they that dwell in the east are *etc.*]
²¹Surely such are the dwellings of the unrighteous,
And this is the place of him that knoweth not God.

Bildad explains this rock that Job would remove from its place (4bc). He refers to the established order of things, in which the wicked suffer for their misdeeds. Job claims to be righteous and wants God to show him to be righteous. But Job is suffering the afflictions that come upon a wicked man, which proves to Bildad that he must be guilty of great wickedness. To declare such a man to be righteous would be to overturn the established moral order of the world. That, as Bildad sees it, is what Job is asking for.

The development of thought includes the following points with regard to the wicked man:

1. His household lights are extinguished (5–6).
2. He is entrapped by his own counsel or schemes (7–11).
3. The conclusion of life (12–14)—strength weakened (12); fatal disease (13); facing "the king of terrors," *i.e.* death (14; *cf.* Psa 49.14; Isa 28.15, 18).
4. Complete extinction of his family and memory (15–19).
5. The horror at his fate (20).

The description concludes with a summary, which again indicates the main theme (21).

The description of the destiny of the wicked (5–21) seems pretty academic. Why is Job so upset and outraged? (19.1–6). Because he realizes Bildad is talking about him! Bildad says "the wicked," but he has Job in mind, and Job knows it (*cf.* 21.27f). Furthermore, Job is not just guessing. The context proves that he is right. What establishes the context are the questions in verse 4. According to Bildad, when Job so fervently expresses a desire for vindication, he wants the entire moral order of the world to be changed for him. The established order of things calls for the wicked to experience the horrors of verses 5–21. Yet the description looks very much like the very horrors that Job is experiencing. It is the suffering of the wicked man. Yet Job protests against it, and wishes that he might be declared righteous. As Bildad sees it, Job wants all the established rules to be changed for him. No wonder this righteous man is outraged!

Job's Reply to Bildad (19)

At the end of this round of speeches, Job will directly challenge the view of the wicked man being set forth by the friends (ch 21). But at this moment he is just plain outraged that his friends regard him as a wicked man suffering what is justly due. And, more than that, he complains against God for placing him in this situation which makes him appear to be guilty when he is not. Some of Job's hardest words against God are found in this chapter. Yet Job rises to his highest point of faith at the close of this speech. God is all he has, and he means to hold on to him, no matter what.

Response to the Friends (19.1–6)

Then Job answered and said,
²How long will ye vex my soul,
And break me in pieces with words?
³These ten times have ye reproached me:
Ye are not ashamed that ye deal hardly with me.
⁴And be it indeed that I have erred,
Mine error remaineth with myself.
⁵If indeed ye will magnify yourselves against me,
And plead against me my reproach; [Or, Will ye indeed …reproach?]
⁶Know now that God hath subverted me *in my cause* **[Or, overthrown me],**
And hath compassed me with his net.

Job begins with an impatience (2) that matches Bildad's (18.2a): "How long will you (plural) vex my soul?" The Hebrew verb (S.3013) means "to grieve, to make sad, to afflict" (Ges. 328); "cause grief or sorrow" (BDB 387a). It is rendered "torment" in several versions (RSV, NASB, NKJV and NIV). Then further: "…and break me in pieces (or crush) me with words?" Time after time they have launched their reproaches or insults against him and are not ashamed to be treating him so severely (3). So, for the time being, Job simply brushes aside the argument and complains of the friends' unrelenting prosecution of him.

But even if it were true that he had erred or gone astray, the friends certainly have no knowledge of it and have not proved it (4). Job has challenged them from the beginning: "Teach me …and cause me to understand wherein I have erred" (6.24). But they cannot do so. They infer his guilt from the absolute connection between sin and suffering in their traditional theology. Then they considered his complaints to be evidence of his guilt (*cf.* 15.2–6). But the fact is, they are treating him severely despite having no certain knowledge of his guilt. As Job puts it: "My error remains with me" (4). Only I have knowledge of it.

If they are so determined to rise up against him and to argue his guilt on the ground of his reproach or state of humiliation, referring to the lowly estate to which he has been reduced, Job insists that the real explanation of his suffering is not that he is guilty, but that God, by treating him as guilty when he is not, "has wronged me" (NKJV, NASB, NIV) or "put me in the wrong" (RSV). Thus he claims to be the victim of a perversion of justice (5–6).

The following section expands upon this complaint.

Complaint of Hostile Treatment from God (19.7–12)

⁷Behold, I cry out of wrong [Or, cry out, Violence], but I am not heard:
I cry for help, but there is no justice.
⁸He hath walled up my way that I cannot pass,
And hath set darkness in my paths.
⁹He hath stripped me of my glory,
And taken the crown from my head.
¹⁰He hath broken me down on every side, and I am gone;
And my hope hath he plucked up like a tree.
¹¹He hath also kindled his wrath against me,
And he counteth me unto him as *one of* his adversaries.
¹²His troops come on together,
And cast up their way against me,
And encamp round about my tent.

Caught in God's net (6), Job cried out against such violent treatment, but his cry goes unheard (7a). He screams for help, "but there is no justice" (7b). God has left him no way out of this trap (8). The road is walled up so that he cannot pass, and God has shrouded his paths in darkness so that he cannot see the way to go. Furthermore, God has stripped Job of his reputation for righteousness (9), broken him down and taken away all hope (10). Finally, God has taken up a hostile position against him, regarding Job as an enemy (11–12). So the situation appears to Job.

Consequence of God's Hostility Toward Job: Alienation of All Human Relations (19.13–22)

¹³He hath put my brethren far from me,
And mine acquaintance are wholly estranged from me.
¹⁴My kinsfolk have failed,
And my familiar friends have forgotten me.
¹⁵They that dwell [Or, sojourn] in my house, and my maids, count me for
   a stranger;
I am an alien in their sight.
¹⁶I call unto my servant, and he giveth me no answer,
Though I entreat him with my mouth.

¹⁷My breath is strange to my wife,
And my supplication [Or, I make supplication; Or, I am loathsome] to the
children of mine own mother [Or, of my body].
¹⁸Even young children despise me;
If I arise, they speak against me.
¹⁹All my familiar friends [Heb. *the men of my council*] abhor me,
And they whom I loved are turned against me.
²⁰My bone cleaveth to my skin and to my flesh,
And I am escaped with the skin of my teeth.
²¹Have pity upon me, have pity upon me, O ye my friends;
For the hand of God hath touched me.
²²Why do ye persecute me as God,
And are not satisfied with my flesh?

Job's condition has terrible psychological consequences, including complete isolation from all human relations. God's hostility toward Job manifested in the afflictions has estranged all human relations from him and deprived him of all human sympathy and respect. The estrangement includes his brothers and acquaintances (13), his kinsfolk and intimate friends (14), his household servants (15–16), his wife and "the children of my womb" (literal translation, 17; *cf.* 3.10 for the language), probably meaning "those who had issued from the same womb as himself" (ICC), and young children (18).

Abhorred by his intimate friends and alienated from his loved ones (19), barely alive (20), Job breaks down and begs his friends for pity (21–22). God's hand has touched him with terrible affliction. Why do the friends have to add to his miseries, persecuting him as God has done and not being satisfied at the terrible condition to which his flesh has been reduced? All argument is forgotten for the moment as Job begs the friends for some simple kindness.

Hope for the Future: Confidence of Ultimate Vindication (19.23–29)

²³Oh that my words were now written!
Oh that they were inscribed in a book!
²⁴That with an iron pen and lead
They were graven in the rock for ever!
²⁵But {Or, For} as for me I know that my Redeemer [Or, vindicator: Heb. *goel*]
liveth,
And at last he will stand up upon the earth:

²⁶And after my skin, *even* this *body*, is destroyed,
Then without my flesh shall I see God; [Or, And after my skin hath been thus
    destroyed, yet from my flesh shall I see God]
²⁷Whom I, even I, shall see, on my side,
And mine eyes shall behold, and not as a stranger.
My heart [Heb. *reins*] is consumed within me.
²⁸If ye say, How we will persecute him!
And that the root of the matter is found in me;
²⁹Be ye afraid of the sword:
For wrath *bringeth* [Or, wrathful are] the punishments of the sword,
That ye may know there is a judgment.

Job sees no sign of compassion from the friends. Theology is regarded
as more important than friendship. So he is left with God alone. But he
simply cannot believe that God will continue his hostility forever. He
who is his adversary now will ultimately be his vindicator. The section
has three parts:

1. *Longing for a Permanent Record of His Protestations of Innocence (23–
24).* The reproaches of the friends would no doubt continue after Job's
death. Job cannot bear the thought that their accusations would go un-
challenged and his own memory be preserved as that of a great sinner. If
only a permanent record of his words, especially his claim to have been
wronged and his cry for matters to be set right (5–7), might continue
to defend his integrity and at least put up a challenge to their charges
against him!

2. *Confidence of Ultimate Vindication (25–27).* But Job wants more
than opportunity to continue after his death to challenge the accusations against him through his own written testimony (23–24). He wants
vindication! He expects to die without being vindicated. But he is confident that his Redeemer (Heb. *goel*, vindicator) is living and will ultimately arise to take his part and set things right (25). After the corruption of his body, he is confident he will see God, not as an adversary as
at present, but on his side and "not as a stranger"—*i.e.*, estranged, hostile
(26–27). Job is almost overcome with emotion as he considers the prospect (27c).

The identity of the Redeemer has been disputed. But surely the reference is to God, whom Job expects to see. Since God has been represented
as "Job's adversary rather than defender" (in 7–12), AB thinks some other
figure, perhaps to be identified as an umpire (9.33) or witness (16.19) dis-

tinct from God, must be intended. But, early on, Job has already wished for a time when God would change his attitude toward him (14.13–15).

Job has had no revelation from God, of course, but he is struggling to hold on to God. The conviction expressed here that a man would indeed live after death (an advance on the views expressed in 14.13–15 and 16.18–17.3) is the highest peak to which Job's faith rises. But this conviction is not grounded upon a revelation from God. It arises from Job's reasoning grounded on faith in God and his understanding of the character of God. God could not leave matters as they were. God, being who he is (*cf.* Gen 18.25), would simply have to act and to set things right, if not in this life, then after death. But it is Jesus Christ who, by his teaching and then his resurrection from the dead, provides the evidence that this instinct and conviction concerning which Job has struggled is correct. See further the summary at the end of Round Two of the debate.

3. Closing Threat to the Friends (28–29). The closing verses have links to two previous passages in this chapter. First, the assertion that the friends have not exposed sin in him; if he has erred, the error remains hidden within himself (4). Second, the plea for pity from the friends, in which Job demands to know why they continued to persecute him just as God himself has done (21f). At the end Job sees no sign of pity from the friends and anticipates that they will be determined to continue their persecution on the ground that the root of the matter is in Job (28). They would continue to function as a kind of inquisition, determined to torture a confession from Job.

Job, therefore, closes with a threat to the friends, which is itself a strong expression of his faith in God and his justice. If the friends continue to persecute him and to falsely accuse him, Job warns them that they must beware the sword of divine judgment, which will be turned against them when his Vindicator arises to establish his innocence (29).

This man may feel that his paths lie in darkness (8). He may complain of mistreatment at the hands of God (7–12). But he cannot give God up, and he stedfastly continues to place confidence in the justice of God.

Zophar's Second Speech: The Portion of the Wicked (20)

Zophar tries his hand at expounding upon the second round theme of the friends but with a new emphasis (4f). Verse 29 summarizes Zophar's speech and thereby indicates the subject of the chapter.

Brief Preface: Justification for Speaking (20.1–3)

Zophar is stung by Job's reproof of himself and the other friends. He is indignant that Job shows so little respect for the "comfort" he and his colleagues have provided. Recall that Job's first stinging reproof had followed Zophar's first speech. He responded to Zophar with bitter sarcasm (12.2f) and in the same speech called the friends "forgers of lies" and quack physicians (13.4), said their wisdom would be to hush their mouths (13.5), threatened them with judgment for showing partiality toward God (13.7–11), and dismissed their arguments as worthless (13.12). Clearly he has lost confidence in the friends, and the same harsh criticism continues in his later speeches, in which he says their comfort only increased his misery, calls them windbags, and expresses wonder that they will not just hush (16.2f); their hearts are hidden from understanding (17.4); they are betrayers of a friend, who deserve a severe curse (17.5); they ought to be ashamed of the way they dealt with him (19:2f), their accusations against him only exposing their own ignorance (19.4). He closed his last speech with a threat: if they keep on persecuting him they have reason to fear the sword of divine judgment (19.28f).

Wow! No wonder Zophar is upset. Stirred to a moral indignation by Job's reproof, and perhaps especially the closing threat, Zophar speaks out of the spirit of his understanding, which provides him with an answer.

Then answered Zophar the Naamathite, and said,
²Therefore do my thoughts give answer to me,
Even by reason of my haste that is in me [Or, And by reason of *this* my haste
is within me].
³I have heard the reproof which putteth me to shame;
And the spirit of my understanding answereth me [Or, But out of my
understanding my spirit answereth me].

A Wicked Man's Portion From God (20.4–29)

The heading comes from the summary at the end (29). Zophar's speech is the third verse of the same old song, except for a new slant at the beginning (4f).

⁴Knowest thou *not* this of old time,
Since man was placed upon earth,
⁵That the triumphing of the wicked is short,

And the joy of the godless but for a moment?
⁶Though his height mount up to the heavens,
And his head reach unto the clouds;
⁷Yet he shall perish for ever like his own dung:
They that have seen him shall say, Where is he?
⁸He shall fly away as a dream, and shall not be found:
Yea, he shall be chased away as a vision of the night.
⁹The eye which saw him shall see him no more;
Neither shall his place any more behold him.
¹⁰His children shall seek the favor of the poor [Or as otherwise read, *The poor
   shall oppress his children*],
And his hands shall give back his wealth.
¹¹His bones are full of his youth,
But it shall lie down with him in the dust.
¹²Though wickedness be sweet in his mouth,
Though he hide it under his tongue,
¹³Though he spare it, and will not let it go,
But keep it still within his mouth;
¹⁴Yet his food in his bowels is turned,
It is the gall of asps within him.
¹⁵He hath swallowed down riches, and he shall vomit them up again;
God will cast them out of his belly.
¹⁶He shall suck the poison of asps:
The viper's tongue shall slay him.
¹⁷He shall not look upon the rivers,
The flowing streams of honey and butter.
¹⁸That which he labored for shall he restore, and shall not swallow it down;
According to the substance that he hath gotten [Heb. *of his exchange*], he
   shall not rejoice.
¹⁹For he hath oppressed and forsaken the poor;
He hath violently taken away a house, and he shall not build it up [Or, which
   he builded not].
²⁰Because he knew no quietness within him [Or, in his greed: Heb. *in his belly*],
He shall not save aught of that wherein he delighteth.
²¹There was nothing left that he devoured not;
Therefore his prosperity shall not endure.
²²In the fulness of his sufficiency he shall be in straits:
The hand of every one that is in misery shall come upon him.
²³When he is about to fill his belly [Or, Let it be for the filling of his belly that
   God shall cast *etc.*], *God* will cast the fierceness of his wrath upon him,
And will rain it upon him while he is eating [Or, as his food].

²⁴He shall flee from the iron weapon,
And the bow of brass shall strike him through.
²⁵He draweth it forth, and it cometh out of his body;
Yea, the glittering point cometh out of his gall:
Terrors are upon him.
²⁶All darkness is laid up for his treasures:
A fire not blown *by man* shall devour him;
It shall consume that which is left in his tent [Or, It shall go ill with him that
    is left].
²⁷The heavens shall reveal his iniquity,
And the earth shall rise up against him.
²⁸The increase of his house shall depart;
His goods shall flow away in the day of his wrath.
²⁹This is the portion of a wicked man from God,
And the heritage appointed unto him by God.

1. The Triumph of the Wicked Short (4–11). Zophar seems to be attempting a reply to Job's complaint about the prosperity of the wicked (*cf.* 9.24; 12.6). He seems to concede that the wicked may prosper for a while, but his triumph is brief. He claims that this point has been known from "of old time," ever since man has been on the earth (4f). No matter to what heights he may rise, the wicked man "shall perish for ever" (6–7a), and all trace of his existence shall vanish (7b–9). His children will be left impoverished, for his wealth must be returned (10). He will go to the grave with youthful vigor still in his bones (11).

2. The Return of His Wealth (12–19) …elaboration of verse 10b. The wicked man must give up what he has taken by evil means (*cf.* 19). His wickedness, likely referring to his ill-gotten gains ("riches" in 15, acquired by evil doing), is compared to food that is tasty in the mouth, so much so that he would like to keep it there, but turns bad in the stomach (12–14). So he must vomit up the riches he has swallowed, casting them out of his belly (15). Thus he will not be able to enjoy his wealth, which has been stolen or extorted from the poor and helpless (16–19).

3. The Wicked Filled With Divine Wrath (20–29). His greed (20–21) will be satisfied all right. God will fill him …with his judgments (22–28). Zophar concludes with a summary statement: Such is the portion which a wicked man receives from God (29).

Job's Reply to Zophar: The Friends' Second Round Speeches Directly Challenged (21)

In the second round of speeches, each of the friends argued more or less the same thesis with regard to "the portion of a wicked man from God." Job was outraged. Their description of the afflictions of a wicked man were just such as Job himself was suffering. They said "the wicked man" or "a wicked man," but they were thinking of him, and Job knew it (*cf.* 21.27f). So he was outraged that they would think such things of him, who was so conscious of his own piety. His first two second round responses (chs 16–17 and 19) began by taking the friends to task, and then continued by complaining that God had placed him in such a situation. But to this point he has not directly challenged their basic premise concerning the afflictions of a wicked man. Now he does. After each of the friends has taken his turn, in this third reply Job directly challenges their position, finally responding to the position argued by the friends all through the second round of speeches. His introduction (in 2–6) seems calmer, less expressive of personal outrage, perhaps because he is making reply to the issue and not so much venting anger against a personal offence.

Introduction Preparing the Friends for the Shocking Facts to be Presented (21.2–6)

Then Job answered and said,
²Hear diligently my speech;
And let this be your consolations.
³Suffer me, and I also will speak;
And after that I have spoken, mock on [Or, thou shalt mock].
⁴As for me, is my complaint to [Or, of] man?
And why should I not be impatient?
⁵Mark me [Heb. *Look unto me*], and be astonished,
And lay your hand upon your mouth.
⁶Even when I remember I am troubled,
And horror taketh hold on my flesh.

Job begins by asking for careful attention to his words, which would be the consolation of the friends (2), since they seemed to be unable to provide any other. Permit me to speak, he pleads, and then you can continue your mockery (3). Job's complaint is not "to man" or "of man," implying, rather, to or of God; and he feels he has good reason for impatience (4). He prepares the friends by advising them in advance that the facts he has to present will be downright shocking (5–6). He expects them to be shocked (5), and he himself is greatly disturbed when he thinks of these facts (6).

Prosperity of the Wicked (21.7–16)

⁷Wherefore do the wicked live,
Become old, yea, wax mighty in power?
⁸Their seed is established with them in their sight,
And their offspring before their eyes.
⁹Their houses are safe from fear [Or, in peace, without fear],
Neither is the rod of God upon them.
¹⁰Their bull gendereth, and faileth not;
Their cow calveth, and casteth not her calf.
¹¹They send forth their little ones like a flock,
And their children dance.
¹²They sing [Heb. *lift up* the voice] to the timbrel and harp,
And rejoice at the sound of the pipe.
¹³They spend their days in prosperity,
And in a moment they go down to Sheol.
¹⁴And they say unto God, Depart from us;
For we desire not the knowledge of thy ways.
¹⁵What is the Almighty, that we should serve him?
And what profit should we have, if we pray unto him?
¹⁶Lo [Or, *Ye say*, Lo *etc.*], their prosperity is not in their hand:
The counsel of the wicked is far from me.

The position of the friends simply does not square with the facts. In view of their position, Job raises a question: Why do the wicked prosper? (7). He then continues by pointing out that the wicked do in fact prosper, live joyful lives and then "in a moment go down to Sheol" (8–13)—*i.e.*, not with the drawn out agony that he was experiencing—all in spite of the godlessness of their lives (14f). In fact, their prosperity comes from God, Job implies in 16a.

After such shocking words Job finds it necessary to issue a disclaimer (16b). "The counsel of the wicked" summarized in 14f does not represent his view. Job does not understand why the wicked often prosper (7). But admitting the fact of their prosperity does not mean that he has adopted the philosophy that there is no advantage or profit in serving and praying to God.

Calamity Upon the Wicked Not Regular But Exceptional (21.17–26)

¹⁷How oft is it that the lamp of the wicked is put out?

That their calamity cometh upon them? [Or, How oft is the lamp of the
wicked put out, and *how oft* cometh their calamity upon them?
God distributeth sorrows in his anger. They are as stubble …away]

That *God* distributeth sorrows in his anger?

¹⁸That they are as stubble before the wind,

And as chaff that the storm carrieth away?

¹⁹*Ye say,* God layeth up his iniquity for his children.

Let him recompense it unto himself, that he may know it [Or, God layeth up
his iniquity for his children: he rewardeth him, and he shall know it. His
eyes shall see his destruction, and he shall drink *etc.*]:

²⁰Let his own eyes see his destruction,

And let him drink of the wrath of the Almighty.

²¹For what careth he for his house after him,

When the number of his months is cut off?

²²Shall any teach God knowledge,

Seeing he judgeth those that are high?

²³One dieth in his full strength,

Being wholly at ease and quiet:

²⁴His pails are full of milk,

And the marrow of his bones is moistened.

²⁵And another dieth in bitterness of soul,

And never tasteth of good.

²⁶They lie down alike in the dust,

And the worm covereth them.

The questions in verses 17f relate to Bildad's claim (in 18.5f). Bildad began
his exposition of the calamities that come upon the wicked by saying his
light shall be put out. Job challenges Bildad's assertion. How often does
that happen? he asks. True, the wicked sometimes experience calamity,
but not regularly or even frequently (17f).

Then verses 19–21 seem to be a response to Zophar's assertion about
the impoverishment of the wicked man's children (20.10). Most versions
interpret verse 19a as citing a view of the friends. But that is not directly
said: "You say" (or the like) is lacking from the text. On the other hand,
the same result can be obtained by punctuating 19a as a question: "Does
God lay up his iniquity for his children?" Job considers the question,
whether the wicked man's punishment may be reserved for his children,
and replies that the suffering of his children after his death is no punish-

ment for him (19–21). The punishment should fall upon him personally, since he does not care what happens to his household once he is dead and gone.

Job charges the friends with making themselves wiser than God (apparently the meaning of verse 22). They have not been describing what is, but what they think ought to be. The fact is, whatever differences of fortune may exist among men in life, they all come to the same end (23–26). The implication may be: If the wicked man is not punished in life, he is no worse off than the godly man.

Answer to the Friends' Insinuations Against Him:
Their Position With Regard to the Final End of the Wicked Not
Consistent With the Facts (21.27–34)

²⁷Behold, I know your thoughts,
And the devices wherewith ye would wrong me.
²⁸For ye say, Where is the house of the prince?
And where is the tent wherein the wicked dwelt?
²⁹Have ye not asked wayfaring men?
And do ye not know their evidences,
³⁰That the evil man is reserved to the day of calamity [Or, spared in *etc.*]?
That they are led forth to the day of wrath [Or, led away in *etc.*]?
³¹Who shall declare his way to his face?
And who shall repay him what he hath done?
³²Yet shall he be borne to the grave,
And men shall keep watch over the tomb. [Or, Moreover he is borne to the grave, and keepeth watch over his tomb. The clods of the valley are sweet unto him; and all men draw *etc.*]
³³The clods of the valley shall be sweet unto him,
And all men shall draw after him,
As there were innumerable before him.
³⁴How then comfort ye me in vain,
Seeing in your answers there remaineth *only* falsehood?

Job understands the insinuations of the friends against him in their questions about the wicked (27f). But Job contends that the view of the friends is grounded upon extremely limited experience. Their view does not agree with the evidence provided by travelers who have seen a lot of the world. They give a wholly different account of the fate of the wicked (29f). Their testimony would be that the wicked often escape the day of calamity and wrath (30). The power of the wicked man is such that no one holds him responsible for his conduct in life (31). Then at death he has an honorable burial, a peaceful rest, and is followed to the grave by all men, just as countless others have gone before him (32–33). Verse 33 seems to mean that his experience at the end is no different from that of all other men.

That being the case, what comfort can they expect Job to find in words so full of falsehood? (34).

Important Developments in the Second Round of Speeches

The second round of speeches (chs 15–21) produced two main developments. On the one hand, the physical suffering and, even more, the appearance of guilt associated with that suffering, have subjected Job to a severe trial of faith. He felt alienated from God and isolated from humanity as well. Under the pressures of the debate, he felt God was acting as an enemy toward him (16.6–17); he accused God of injustice in his own case (19.5–12); and, in reply to the friends' persistent effort to lump his sufferings with those of wicked and godless men, he complained that, in fact, the wicked often seem to prosper, never being brought to justice (ch 21). The second round of speeches ended with the fullest statement of the great moral problem which Job's sufferings and the debate with the friends brought into such sharp focus.

On the other hand, Job rose to his highest point of faith in this round (19.23–29). It is a good time to pause and trace his progress. After the hopelessness of his first replies to Eliphaz (chs 6–7) and Bildad (chs 9–10), and having lost confidence in getting help from his friends, Job expressed the wish that he might be able to take his case to God himself (13.3) and the determination to defend his integrity before God, no matter what the consequence (13.13–19). That, at least, showed a confidence in the justice of God.

After the assertion that man does not even have the hope of a tree (14.7–12), Job expressed the wish that it might be otherwise—*i.e.*, that God would preserve him in Sheol, appointing some future time to call for him and to hear his case (14.13–15). That was when he raised the possibility: "If a man die, shall he live?"

Then he expressed the wish that his blood might remain uncovered after his death, continuing to cry out for vindication (16.18), and the confidence that he had a witness in heaven who would eventually speak up for him and establish his innocence (16.19–21). He pleaded for a pledge from God that it might be done (17.3). Still, this second answer to Eliphaz ended in despair (17.11–16).

But then his second reply to Bildad closed with the wish that his words protesting his innocence might be permanently engraven on rock (19.23f) and the conviction that his Redeemer or Vindicator lived and would eventually stand up to take his side and to vindicate him (19.25–27).

We must remember that Job has had no revelation from God. Job has reasoned his way from the wish that he might live again after his death to the certain conviction that it would be. His faith in God and his understanding of the character of God demands it. God simply cannot leave matters as they are. At some time in the future, even after death, God will have to act and to set things right. But Jesus Christ will provide the proof. The resurrection of Jesus Christ from the dead will provide the certain confirmation. Jesus will prove that the instinct and the conviction to which Job has struggled is exactly right.

So, on the one hand, Job's complaints have demonstrated the greatness of his trial. On the other, his expressions of faith reveal a sheer determination to hold on to God, no matter what.

Third Round of Speeches: Conclusion of the Debate (Job 22–28)

Arguments based on the general conception of God (First Round) and the fate of the wicked man (Second Round) have been exhausted, without bringing Job to a conviction of sin or to confess his guilt. Job is more adamant than ever in his insistence upon his innocence and his contention that he has been wronged by God and, in fact, that something is out of whack in the way the world is being run. Nothing remains to the friends but to charge Job directly with great sins.

Job's speeches put pressure on the friends to that very end. He challenged them from the beginning to show him his error (6.24f). He asserted that they have no knowledge of his error, even if he has erred (19.4). Finally, he exposed the tendency and implication of the speeches about the life and destiny of the wicked. You are using these speeches about the wicked man to wrong me, he said. You speak of the wicked, but you are referring to me (21.27f).

In the Third Round the veil is cast off and Eliphaz speaks directly of the sins of which he imagines Job to be guilty.

Eliphaz' Third Speech: Job Charged With Specific Sins (22)

Explanation of Job's Afflictions (22.1–11)

Then answered Eliphaz the Temanite, and said,
²Can a man be profitable unto God?
Surely he that is wise is profitable unto himself.
³Is it any pleasure to the Almighty, that thou art righteous?
Or is it gain *to him*, that thou makest thy ways perfect?
⁴Is it for thy fear *of him* [Or, for fear of thee] that he reproveth thee,
That he entereth with thee into judgment?
⁵Is not thy wickedness great?
Neither is there any end to thine iniquities.
⁶For thou hast taken pledges of thy brother for nought,
And stripped the naked of their clothing.
⁷Thou hast not given water to the weary to drink,
And thou hast withholden bread from the hungry.
⁸But as for the mighty man [Or, the man of arm], he had the earth [Or, land];
And the honorable man [Heb. *he whose person is accepted*], he dwelt in it.
⁹Thou hast sent widows away empty,
And the arms of the fatherless have been broken.
¹⁰Therefore snares are round about thee,
And sudden fear troubleth thee,
¹¹Or darkness, so that thou canst not see,
And abundance of waters cover thee. [Or, Or dost thou not see the darkness,
   And the flood of waters that covereth thee?]

1. Argument: Job's Afflictions Can Only be Due to His Sins (2–5). Eliphaz is ready to charge Job with specific sins. But he has no knowledge of Job's guilt. On what ground can he charge him with sin? An introduction (2–5) sets forth the grounds on which he is convinced Job must be guilty. He considers the reason for Job's suffering and concludes that only sin and wickedness can account for it.

Job's afflictions are regarded as a divine reproof and a matter of God entering into judgment with Job (4). In fact, Eliphaz' view from the beginning has been that such afflictions are a chastisement, a reproof or correction (5.17). But now he discusses the reason for such chastisement or reproof. The first point Eliphaz wants laid to rest is that God may have some selfish or ulterior motive for such chastisement. He reasons that God receives no advantage or benefit from man's conduct (2–3). The benefit of wisdom and righteousness is to the man himself. This reasoning seems to imply that God could have no selfish or ulterior motive for such corrective afflictions. The reason for the afflictions cannot be found in God, but must be found within the man.

But why then does God bring such chastisement on Job? Is it because of his piety? (4). That is absurd; it makes no sense at all. Therefore the divine corrective action can only be due to Job's sins (5). Eliphaz has not witnessed such sins. He does not know Job to be guilty. He has simply convinced himself on the basis of the reasoning in verses 2–5 that no other conclusion is possible.

2. Specific Charges Against Job (6–9). But if Job's sufferings are due to his sins, what are those sins? Eliphaz thinks he knows. He names specific sins of which he thinks Job is probably guilty. Of course, he has no knowledge or proof that Job is guilty of these sins. But for the reason given (in 2–5) he thinks Job must be guilty of something. So he suggests a list of sins such as a man like Job would likely be guilty. They are such sins as a powerful man, someone who possessed a great deal of land and lived in it (8), might well be guilty.

But Eliphaz is only guessing. He does not know. He thinks Job may well be guilty of such neglect of duty, which would explain his troubles. But he does not ask Job whether he might be guilty of such sins. He asserts that he is. Eliphaz is guilty of outrageous false accusation, which is directly traceable to his arrogant and foolish commitment to a false theology, which he holds at the expense of simple justice.

3. Job's Afflictions the Consequence of Such Sins (10–11). "Therefore" introduces this conclusion from Eliphaz' reasoning.

Warning About the Counsel of the Wicked (22.12–20)

¹²Is not God in the height of heaven?
And behold the height [Heb. *head*] of the stars, how high they are!
¹³And thou sayest, What doth God know?
Can he judge through the thick darkness?
¹⁴Thick clouds are a covering to him, so that he seeth not;
And he walketh on the vault of heaven.
¹⁵Wilt thou keep [Or, Dost thou mark] the old way
Which wicked men have trodden?
¹⁶Who were snatched away before their time,
Whose foundation was poured out as a stream,
¹⁷Who said unto God, Depart from us;
And, What can the Almighty do for [Or, to] us [Heb. *them*]?

¹⁸Yet he filled their houses with good things:
But the counsel of the wicked is far from me.
¹⁹The righteous see it, and are glad;
And the innocent laugh them to scorn,
²⁰*Saying*, Surely they that did rise up against us are cut off,
And the remnant of them [Or, that which remained to them; Or, their
    abundance] the fire hath consumed.

Eliphaz indicts Job for the thinking which he imagines to be behind Job's sins. Job has adopted the counsel of the wicked and follows their path.

1. Job Quoted (12–14). God is so far above the earth! (12). Eliphaz imagines Job thinking God cannot see through the covering of clouds so as to be aware of human behavior on earth (13–14).

2. Warning Against Following the Counsel of the Wicked (15–18). The view Eliphaz imagines Job taking is an ungodly one, of course. It is the way of the wicked. So Eliphaz goes on to ask Job whether he would walk in the old way trod by wicked men who experience premature death (15–16). He further describes such men as dismissing God, thinking he can do nothing to or for them, in spite of the fact that he blessed them with wonderful blessings (17–18a). At this point Eliphaz inserts the same disclaimer (18b) that Job himself had asserted (21.16b).

Job had trodden on dangerous ground in 21.2–16. He himself recognized the possibility of being misunderstood, and therefore issued the disclaimer with regard to "the counsel of the wicked" (21.16b). Now it appears that Eliphaz has drawn the very conclusion about Job which Job had wanted to prevent by his disclaimer. In any case, Eliphaz is warning Job that he was walking in the way of wicked men who are punished for such impiety.

3. Role of the Righteous at the Judgment on the Wicked (19–20). Eliphaz warns that Job is adopting the godless thinking that brings judgment on wicked men. The righteous, however, see the downfall of their evil oppressors and rejoice. Verses 19–20 are thus connected with verse 16.

Exhortation and Promises (22.21–30)

²¹Acquaint now thyself with him, and be at peace:
Thereby good shall come unto thee [Or as otherwise read, Thereby shall
    thine increase be good].
²²Receive, I pray thee, the law [Or, instruction] from his mouth,
And lay up his words in thy heart.
²³If thou return to the Almighty, thou shalt be built up,

If thou put away unrighteousness far from thy tents [Or, Thou shalt put
away… and shalt lay up].
²⁴And lay thou *thy* treasure [Or, ore] in the dust [Or, on the earth],
And *the gold of* Ophir among the stones of the brooks;
²⁵And the Almighty will be thy treasure,
And precious silver unto thee [Or, precious silver shall be thine].
²⁶For then shalt thou delight thyself in the Almighty,
And shalt lift up thy face unto God.
²⁷Thou shalt make thy prayer unto him, and he will hear thee;
And thou shalt pay thy vows.
²⁸Thou shalt also decree a thing, and it shall be established unto thee;
And light shall shine upon thy ways.
²⁹When they cast *thee* down [Or, are made low], thou shalt say, *There is
lifting up;*
And the humble person [Heb. *him that is lowly of eyes*] he will save.
³⁰He will deliver *even* him that is not innocent:
Yea, he shall be delivered through the cleanness of thy hands.

Eliphaz concludes with an exhortation to return to God in view of the
bright prospects that would surely be Job's if he repents. The exhortation
to return to God and put away unrighteousness (23) includes an implication of greed on Job's part. He must rid himself of trust in treasure
(24), the result being that God would be his treasure (25). He must delight himself in the Almighty and pray with the assurance of being heard
(26–27). His purposes would be established (contrast Isa 7.5–7) and light
would shine upon his ways (28). When men are cast down, Job would be
able to encourage them with assurance of elevation, and God would save
the lowly (29). Even the person who is not innocent would be delivered
through the power of Job's intercession (30).

Evaluation

Eliphaz again shows himself to be good-hearted and well-intended. He
makes a wonderful evangelistic-type appeal for Job's repentance. The
problem is, it is all irrelevant. He cannot speak to Job's case because he
has no room in his theology for a suffering righteous man. He does not
believe there could be such a thing.

On the other hand, this theology is at the root of the outrageous false
accusation against Job. We cannot be surprised if Job is despondent and
bitter [perhaps better: antagonistic] as he responds to Eliphaz.

Job's Reply (23–24)

Job is outraged. He does not immediately respond to Eliphaz' baseless accusations, though he will in his final speech (ch 31). For the time being they are ignored as Job dwells upon a matter of greater concern, the mysterious divine providence that has made him vulnerable to such accusations. But by now Job knows he can get no satisfaction from the friends and that his only hope of vindication is to take his case to a higher court. The speech takes the form of a soliloquy, not being directly addressed either to the friends or to God. It falls into two main parts:

The Problem of the Darkness (23)

The heading is derived from the last verse of the chapter. Eliphaz spoke of the darkness that enshrouded Job, which kept him from seeing, as a consequence of his sins (22.11). If Job would "return to the Almighty" (22.23), Eliphaz assured him, "light shall shine upon your ways" (22.28). Well, Job could certainly admit to being in darkness, and he refers to this darkness at the end of chapter 23 (v 17). In large measure, this chapter explores the problem of this darkness.

Eliphaz also referred to the darkness in his summary of what he imagined to be the thinking behind Job's sins. He imagined Job thinking God could not see through the thick darkness and the veil of clouds that concealed human conduct from him (22.13f). But that is not what I think at all, Job responds in effect (23.12). The problem is not that darkness conceals my conduct from God. The problem is the darkness that hides God from me.

Job's Complaint (23.1–2)

Then Job answered and said,
²Even to-day is my complaint rebellious [Or, bitter; or *accounted* rebellion]:
My stroke is heavier than my groaning.

If Eliphaz entertained any expectation that Job would submit to his accusations, confess his sins and humble himself before God, he is badly mistaken and doomed to disappointment. Job is determined to defend his personal integrity to the end, and he quickly disabuses Eliphaz' mind of any notion that this inquisition could produce a confession from him. "Even today my complaint is rebellion," he begins (2a). Not submission, but rebellion! That is what you can expect from me, says Job.

He continues: "My hand is heavy upon my groaning" (2b). Commentators have considered two views. *My hand* may mean *the hand on me* (NIV margin), referring to the hand of God that is heavy upon him (*cf.* 1 Sam 5.6, 11b; Psa 32.4). Some therefore try to derive from 2b a meaning along the lines of 6.2–3. But the line is difficult, and I am not sure. *My groaning* is the object, and Peake's suggestion may be on the right track: "My complaint is rebellious, though I do what I can to repress it."

God's Hiddenness and Inaccessibility (23.3–9)

³Oh that I knew where I might find him!
That I might come even to his seat!
⁴I would set my cause in order before him,
And fill my mouth with arguments.
⁵I would know the words which he would answer me,
And understand what he would say unto me.
⁶Would he contend with me in the greatness of his power?
Nay; but he would give heed unto me [Or, he would only give heed].
⁷There the upright might reason with him;
So should I be delivered for ever from my judge.
⁸Behold, I go forward, but he is not *there*;
And backward, but I cannot perceive him;
⁹On the left hand, when he doth work, but I cannot behold him;
He hideth himself on the right hand, that I cannot see him.

Eliphaz counseled Job to "return to the Almighty" (22.23), to which Job replies: I wish I knew where to find him (3a). He longed to approach God's throne, so that he could plead his case with God and hear what his answer would be (3b–5). Going a step beyond chapter 9, Job expresses confidence that God would not simply overwhelm him with power, but, rather, really listen to his case (6). In such circumstances "the upright might reason with him" and thus be vindicated, "delivered for ever from my judge" (7).

But one must find God first (3). As matters stand, God is hidden from Job, who cannot find him anywhere, no matter what direction he looks (8–9).

God's Unaffected Oneness (23.10–17)

¹⁰But [Or, For] he knoweth the way that I take [Heb. *the way that is with me*];
When he hath tried me, I shall come forth as gold.
¹¹My foot hath held fast to his steps;

His way have I kept, and turned not aside.
¹²I have not gone back from the commandment of his lips;
I have treasured up the words of his mouth more than my necessary food
    [Or, portion. See Prov 30.8]. [Or, more than my own law.]
¹³But he is in one *mind* [Or, he is one], and who can turn him?
And what his soul desireth, even that he doeth.
¹⁴For he performeth that which is appointed for me:
And many such things are with him.
¹⁵Therefore am I terrified at his presence;
When I consider, I am afraid of him.
¹⁶For God hath made my heart faint,
And the Almighty hath terrified me;
¹⁷Because I was not cut off before the darkness,
Neither did he cover the thick darkness from my face. [Or, For I am not
    dismayed because of the darkness, nor because thick darkness covereth
    my face.]

1. Protestation of Innocence (10–12). Job may not be able to find God (3, 8f). But God certainly knows all about Job's life, "the way that is with me" (literal translation). Job is under no such illusion as Eliphaz imagined him entertaining (22.12–14). God knows my way, Job well understands (10a); and Job is confident for that very reason that he will emerge from the present trial "as gold," having survived every test (10b). His foot has kept to God's way (11). And despite the implications of Eliphaz' exhortation (22.22), he has not turned from God's commandment, and he has treasured up his words more than his appointed portion of food (12).

2. God's Unchangeableness (13–14). The first line is a problem, but I am deciding for the translation defended in Anderson, which appears in ASV margin and substantially in NASB, NIV, NKJV and NRSV: *But God is one,* followed by the question: *and who can turn him?* (13a). He does not consult counsellors but acts alone. He does as he pleases (13b). *He performs that which is appointed for me* (14a). No one can influence what he does. He just does it. When Job then adds: *And many such things are with him* (14b), perhaps he is leading up to the general application of the principle in Chapter 24. It is not just Job that is affected.

3. Consequence: Terror in the Presence of God (15–17). By now the boldness and confidence Job had expressed (3–7, esp. 6) has been lost. It is the arbitrariness describes as characterizing God, the uncontrolled power, unaffected by human action, that terrifies him and makes him shrink from God's presence (15–16).

None of the experts have worked out verse 17 with much confidence. KJV, ASV and NKJV seem to take it as adding to Job's explanation of his terror: *Because I was not cut off before the darkness, etc.* The darkness could be explained by 3, 8f (*cf.* 22.11; contrast 22.28b). In that case, this reference to the darkness sounds the keynote of the chapter. The reason for his terror is that he was not cut off before the darkness came upon him. But many other possibilities have been suggested, none persuading all.

Complaint That Judgment is Not Brought Against the Evils of the World (Job 24)

Job complained that he cuold not find God, so that he might argue his case before him and get justice for himself (ch 23). But the problem, as Job saw it, was greater than that. More is involved than his own case. The problem of suffering and injustice is widespread. So much evil and op-pression is found in the world, and God does nothing about it (12c). Why, Job asks, does the Almighty not set times for judgment to be manifested against the evil and the oppressors, so that those who know God can see it? (24.1). Thus the direct challenge to the friends' position on the judgment of the wicked in this life, which Job initiated in chapter 21, is continued in chapter 24.

The Manifest Lack of Judgment on Wicked Oppressors (1–12)

The Key Question (24.1)

Why are times not laid up by the Almighty?
And why do not they that know him see his days? [Or, Why is it, seeing times are not hidden from the Almighty, that they who know him see not his days?]

Verse 1 (along with 12c) is the key question that establishes the context. But what is the question? The KJV seems to make it a question of why, since times are not hidden from God, the godly do not see his days, re-ferring to the days when he brings judgment against such evil doers as described in verses 2–12. But the problem, which Job already posed in chapter 21, is not why godly men do not perceive God's judgments, but why those judgments are not exercised by God. The world is filled with evil and oppression (24.2–12), but God does not charge men with folly (12c). So it seems to Job.

Verse 1a is, therefore, better translated with ASV (*cf.* NASB, RSV, and NIV): Why are times not laid up by the Almighty? True, the verb could mean hidden (as in Jer 16.17 and Job 14.13). But it can also mean laid up, as one might hide and thus store up a treasure. So this same verb is used in 15.20, 20.26 and 21.19. So the question is: Why does the Almighty not lay up or keep in reserve times, referring to "times of judgment" (RSV, an interpretive rendering; NASB margin; NIV)?

The second question (1b) is then: Why do those who know God not see these days when he manifests his justice?

The Conditions That Call for Judgment (24.2–11)

²There are that remove the landmarks;
They violently take away flocks, and feed them.
³They drive away the ass of the fatherless;
They take the widow's ox for a pledge.
⁴They turn the needy out of the way:
The poor [Or, meek] of the earth all hide themselves.
⁵Behold, as wild asses in the desert
They go forth to their work, seeking diligently for food [Heb. *prey*];
The wilderness *yieldeth* them bread for their children.
⁶They cut their [Or, his] provender in the field;
And they glean the vintage of the wicked.
⁷They lie all night naked without clothing,
And have no covering in the cold.
⁸They are wet with the showers of the mountains,
And embrace the rock for want of a shelter.
⁹There are that pluck the fatherless from the breast,
And take a pledge of the poor [Or, take in pledge that which is on the poor];
¹⁰*So that* they go about naked without clothing,
And being hungry they carry the sheaves.
¹¹They make oil within the walls of these men;
They tread *their* winepresses, and suffer thirst.

Job sees many cases in which powerful oppressors perpetrate injustices against the poor and the defenseless. Property is stolen from the poor and the helpless, who are driven into hiding (2–4). The poor have to work so hard to get a mere subsistence. They do not have adequate food, shelter or clothing (5–8). Wicked oppressors take their children and their clothing for a pledge, leaving them unclothed (9–10a). The poor work for such powerful wicked men, carrying their sheaves while they themselves are hungry (10b), and squeezing out their oil and treading their winepresses while they themselves are thirsty (11).

The Unheard Cry of the Suffering (24.12)

¹²**From out of the populous city [Heb.** *city of men*] **men groan,**
And the soul of the wounded crieth out:
Yet God regardeth not the folly.

The cries of the suffering are sent up, but God does nothing about it (12). The verb in 12c means to put, to place or to set. Thus: God does not put folly. He does not ascribe folly to the evils of the world. He does not charge men with folly and bring judgment upon them (*cf.* 1). The point is that God seems to be indifferent to such evils in the world.

Rebels Against the Light (24.13–17)

¹³**These are of them that rebel against the light;**
They know not the ways thereof,
Nor abide in the paths thereof.
¹⁴**The murderer riseth with the light;**
He killeth the poor and needy;
And in the night he is as a thief.
¹⁵**The eye also of the adulterer waiteth for the twilight,**
Saying, No eye shall see me:
And he disguiseth his face [Or, putteth a covering on his face].
¹⁶**In the dark they dig through houses:**
They [Or, which they had marked for themselves] shut themselves up in the
**   day-time;**
They know not the light.
¹⁷**For the morning is to all of them as thick darkness;**
For they know the terrors of the thick darkness. [Or, thick darkness is to all
**   of them as the morning; For they** *etc.*]

The previous section (1–12) dealt with the sufferings of the poor and helpless at the hands of the rich and powerful. This one describes another class of evildoers—those who operate secretly, under cover of darkness. The group includes murderers, thieves and adulterers. This type of activity also argues the case for judgment days in which action would be taken against evildoers.

The Moral Indifference Manifested at the End of Such Evil Persons (24.18–25)

¹⁸**Swiftly they** *pass away* **upon the face of the waters [Or,** *Ye say,* **Swiftly** *etc.* **Heb.** *Swift is he etc.*]**;**
Their portion is cursed in the earth:
They turn not into the way of the vineyards.
¹⁹**Drought and heat consume [Heb.** *violently take away*] **the snow waters:**
So doth **Sheol** *those that* **have sinned.**
²⁰**The womb shall forget him;**
The worm shall feed sweetly on him;
He shall be no more remembered;
And unrighteousness shall be broken as a tree [Or, as a tree; even he that devoureth *etc.*]**.**
²¹**He devoureth the barren that beareth not,**
And doeth not good to the widow.
²²**Yet** *God* **preserveth the mighty by his power:**
He riseth up that hath no assurance of life.
²³*God* **giveth them to be in security, and they rest thereon;**
And [Or, But] his eyes are upon their ways.
²⁴**They are exalted; yet a little while, and they are gone;**
Yea [Or, And when they are *etc.*]**, they are brought low, they are taken out of the way as all others,**
And are cut off as the tops of the ears of grain.
²⁵**And if it be not so now, who will prove me a liar,**
And make my speech nothing worth?

These verses form one of the most difficult sections of the book, and no consensus of opinion has emerged among Old Testament scholars. The great difficulty is that after Job complained that God does not bring judgment on the wicked (vv 1–17), now he speaks of the end of the wicked in terms that sound to many like the very position his friends have supported.

Several solutions to this difficulty have been proposed, though none has commanded universal assent. Some think verses 18–20 cite views of the friends, to which Job then responds (ASV margin). The RSV introduces this subsection with the words, "You say…," but without indicating that these words have been added without the least support in the Hebrew text. The NKJV represents these verses as describing what should happen to the wicked rather than what actually does happen to them: "They should be swift on the face of the waters," *etc.* This "should" is repeated to the end of verse 20 but is italicized throughout to indicate that it is not in the original text. Probably, most critical scholars think, these verses actually contain words of the friends. Zophar has no third speech, and some think this may be his third speech, somehow misplaced in transmission.

My own inclination is to try to understand the text as it stands, rather than speculating about possible dislocations of the text. Is that possible? Evidently the author of the whole book thought so. He places these verses in Job's mouth, and evidently does not consider Job to be taking the same view as his friends, for the very last verse is a challenge: Answer me if you can! (25). So how are these verses to be understood as words of Job at odds with the friends and not a surrender to their views?

What becomes of such evildoers as described in the first seventeen verses? Do they experience a day of judgment against them, some extraordinary punishment inflicted on them?

Attention to two points will, perhaps, distinguish the view taken by Job from the speeches of the friends. Job does not take the view, nor has he ever, that the sinner's end is altogether happy. But perhaps the emphasis in the first line—*Swift is he upon the face of the water* (18a)—falls upon the word swift. He passes swiftly away, leaving his portion to be cursed, having no one to care for it, no longer turning into the way of his vineyards (18bc). He is quickly consumed by Sheol (19), and is not lovingly remembered, not even by the mother that bore him (19; contrast Isa 49.15). But "in a moment they go down to Sheol" (21.13) and experience no greater judgment than is common to man (14.1–6). In general the wicked do not experience the long, drawn out torture such as Job is going through.

Despite their misdeeds, preying upon the defenseless (21) the wicked are preserved in life, arising from a sick bed when they seemed to have no hope (22); they live in security (23); they are exalted (24a); and then after a little while they are taken away "as all others" (24). In other words, no extraordinary punishment is inflicted upon them. They suffer only the evils common to man, and their lives come to an end the same way as the lives of men in general (*cf.* 21.23–26). True, the wicked pass away and are swallowed up by Sheol. But so do all others.

Job closes with a challenge: Prove me wrong if you can! (25). He certainly does not understand himself to be simply parroting the views of the friends.

Final Thought

The debate is rapidly moving toward its conclusion. Job has certainly challenged and exposed the weaknesses of the position defended by the friends. But at what a price! He has described the world as without moral government and left God in a terrible light. Clearly the book cannot end this way, even if Job does win the debate with the friends.

Bildad's Third Speech (25)

The debate is drawing to a close. The friends have nothing new to say. Bildad makes no attempt to respond to the facts set forth by Job in chapter 24, and that despite the challenge with which Job closed (24.25). He addresses only the arrogance of Job's claim to innocence and desire to argue his cause with God (23.3–7; *cf.* ch 9). But his points have been made before (4.17ff; 15.14–16), even by Job himself (9.2ff; 14.4). Plainly he has run out of material. But, in fact, none of the friends has anything more to say. Zophar will not even arise for a third speech. The debate is over. The friends are done.

Government of the Almighty (25.1–3)

Then answered Bildad the Shuhite, and said,
²Dominion and fear are with him;
He maketh peace in his high places.
³Is there any number of his armies?
And upon whom doth not his light arise?

Bildad's points are a response to Job's desire to come before the throne of God and argue his cause, "fill my mouth with arguments," as Job said (23:3f). Absurd! thought Bildad. How inconsistent with the true conditions of that heavenly realm! The government belongs to God; his majesty inspires fear (2a). "He makes peace in his high places" (2b) and has power without limit to enforce the peace: "Is there any number of his armies?" (3).

It is difficult to make out the connection of thought when Bildad progresses from "his armies" (3a) to "his light" (3b): "And upon whom does his light not arise?" Some think "armies" may have some reference to the sun, moon and stars, since the heavenly bodies are often called "the hosts of heaven" (Deut 4.19; 17.3; Psa 33.6; Jer 8.2; Dan 8.10), the word "hosts" being a synonym for "armies." It may refer to the angels, who are also called "the hosts of heaven" (Gen 32.1–2; 1 Kgs 22.19; 2 Chron 18.18; Psa 103.20f; 148.2); notice also the way angels and stars are mentioned together in Job 38.7.

In any case, considering what follows in verses 4–6, God's light would seem to be mentioned as exposing man's guilt.

Vindication Before God Impossible (25.4–6)

⁴How then can man be just with God?
Or how can he be clean that is born of a woman?
⁵Behold, even the moon hath no brightness,
And the stars are not pure in his sight:
⁶How much less man, that is a worm!
And the son of man, that is a worm!

It is pure absurdity to imagine the peace of heaven being disturbed by a man coming to "contend with God" (9.3) as Job proposed (23.3–7). No man can prove his innocence before God (4). God shines with light so bright that the moon and stars pale in comparison and the uncleanness of the stars is exposed (5). How much less can the sins of a puny man escape exposure under the brightness of God's light? (6). It is plainly inconceivable that a mere man could take God on and contend with him.

Thus Bildad does not continue in the way of Eliphaz (22.5–11) to charge Job with specific sins. His point is grounded, rather, on the general sinfulness of mankind.

But as I have shown in the introduction to the chapter, all of his points have been made before, even by Job. It is no wonder that Job's reply begins as it does (26.1–4). Bildad has said nothing that Job himself has not already recognized.

Job's Reply (26)

Emptiness of Bildad's Speech (26.1–4)

Then Job answered and said,
²How hast thou helped him that is without power!
How hast thou saved the arm that hath no strength!
³How hast thou counselled him that hath no wisdom,
And plentifully declared sound knowledge!
⁴To whom hast thou uttered words?
And whose spirit [Heb. *breath*] came forth from thee?

The KJV uses question marks throughout, making Job's tone a challenge to Bildad but not sarcastic. But most other versions punctuate with exclamations, so that Job is lashing out with devastating sarcasm. For, if truth be told, Bildad has been no help at all. Who does he think he is talking to? (4a). Certainly his words teach Job nothing. In fact, Job himself has addressed the very problem (9.2ff; 14.4). The attack continues in 4b, which is best understood sarcastically: Under what inspiration did you make such a brilliant speech?

God's Mighty Power Expanded Upon (26.5–14)

⁵They that are deceased [Or, The shades, Heb. *The Rephaim*] tremble
Beneath the waters and the inhabitants thereof.
⁶Sheol is naked before *God* [Heb. *him*],
And Abaddon [Or, Destruction] hath no covering.
⁷He stretcheth out the north over empty space,
And hangeth the earth upon [Or, over] nothing.
⁸He bindeth up the waters in his thick clouds;
And the cloud is not rent under them.
⁹He incloseth the face of his throne,
And spreadeth his cloud upon it.
¹⁰He hath described a boundary upon the face of the waters,
Unto the confines of light and darkness.
¹¹The pillars of heaven tremble
And are astonished at his rebuke.
¹²He stirreth up [Or, stilleth] the sea with his power,
And by his understanding he smiteth through Rahab.
¹³By his Spirit the heavens are garnished [Heb. *beauty*];
His hand hath pierced the swift [Or, fleeing; Or, gliding] serpent.
¹⁴Lo, these are but the outskirts of his ways:
And how small a whisper [Or, how little a portion] do we hear of him [Or, is heard]!
But the thunder of his power [Or, mighty deeds] who can understand?

Job seems to continue the description of God Bildad began (26.2–3). Some scholars (*e.g.* Rowley, Pope in AB) actually think the passage may be a continuation of Bildad's speech on the omnipotence of God, this part having been misplaced in the process of transmission. For what can be the reason for such a passage from Job?

But the fact is, after Job's opening retort to Bildad (2–4) we are not even surprised to have such words from Job. Job sarcastically mocks Bildad's counseling "him that has no wisdom" (3). Who are you talking to? he asks (4a). Job knows as much as Bildad about the marvels of God's power, and proceeds to demonstrate as much in this passage (5–14), as he did once before (12.1–13.2, where the connection was clearly defined in 13.1–2). Job proves that he can outdo Bildad when it comes to a description of the manifestations of God's mighty power.

Instead of thinking back to Bildad's short speech, however, a previous speech of Job's should be consulted. Job has made this speech before (9.5–12), and, in fact, for the purpose of supporting the very point that now serves as Bildad's principal thesis (25.4): "But how can man be just with God?" (9.2–4). Bildad is just preaching Job's sermon. No wonder Job asks him: Who do you think you are talking to? (26.4a).

As Job now continues, his description of God gives support to the biting sarcasm with which the speech begins. He exposes the absurdity of Bildad's counsel by preaching his own sermon to him. Job knows this sermon better than Bildad does.

A few notes on this section: Verse 5a refers to the dead, and 5b may also refer to "the inhabitants of the netherworld." So indicates Pope (in AB), referring to passages which associate this realm with "a watery abyss" (2 Sam 22.5; Jonah 2; Psa 42.7 and 88.3–7; also comparing Psa 104.6, 124.5 and 136.6).

Sheol (6a) is the realm of the dead, and *Abaddon* (6b) means destruction or ruin. The Hebrew Abaddon is translated into Greek at Revelation 9.11.

A number of the later translations accept a different pointing of the Hebrew text in 9a, which results in putting "the moon" (RSV) or "the full moon" (NASB, NIV) in place of "his throne." The reference is to covering the moon with clouds.

AB argues from the parallelism (in verse 12) for the possible translation *stills* (ASV margin, RSV, NASB) in place of *stirs up* (12a). *Rahab* [KJV, proud) refers to a sea monster (12b; *cf.* Psa 87.4; 89.10; Isa 30.7; 51.9f), as the *serpent* (in 13b) is something seen in the heavens, perhaps a formation of clouds. Put *breath* for *Spirit* in 13a, where reference is to winds clearing the sky of clouds.

The concluding verse (14), however, indicates the frustrating problem with which Job has been tangling. When men like Job and his friends have said all they know about God, all they have seen of his operations in the world, they must confess their limitations. They have heard only a small whisper of him. "Who can understand the thunder of his power?" The problems of divine providence discussed by Job in earlier speeches lie beyond the sphere of human understanding. Divine providence is simply a mystery, hidden away from the human mind. This point is directly asserted in chapter 28.

Additional Speech from Job: A Curse Upon His Enemy (27)

Although Job continues to speak, this speech has a new introduction (1). His reply to Bildad's speech was completed in chapter 26. So it is Zophar's turn to speak. But he does not come forward for a third speech. He has nothing more to say. In fact, as we have seen, Bildad's last speech had contributed nothing new. The debate is over. The friends are done. As explained later (32.1), the friends "ceased to answer Job, because he was righteous in his own eyes"—*i.e.,* they despaired of ever convicting Job of sin. In that state of the case, Job continues.

The headings that appear above chapter 27 in the Bibles I have used in my study put the emphasis on the hopelessness of the ungodly (8f) or the portion of the wicked (13–23). True, a great deal of the attention is devoted to "the portion of a wicked man with (or from) God" (13–23). But that is not the main thrust of this chapter. The context is really established by verse 7: "Let my enemy be as the wicked..." The chapter is a curse on Job's enemy. The long section on "the portion of a wicked man" explains what Job means in verse 7. In effect, Job turns the speeches of the friends against them.

Critical scholars often take the view that this description of "the portion of a wicked man" cannot have come from Job. It sounds too much like the friends. So the critics often believe it comes from the friends; it may be the missing speech of Zophar misplaced in the process of transmission.

But they have no textual evidence for such a view, and the fact is, Job does not differ with the friends about the destiny of the wicked. His complaint is that he suffers the fate one expects a wicked man to experience, his afflictions being testimony from God that makes him appear to be wicked (10.17; 16.8). Thus God has wronged him (19.6; 27.2), while the wicked often appear to escape divine justice.

In chapter 27 Job summarizes the traditional view held in common by him and the friends. But he does so in a context in which he describes the end which ought to come upon one who rises up against him and makes false charges against him. Such a man is wicked and ought to suffer the end appointed for a wicked man. That is the main point of this chapter. But we must come to details and establish the context.

Introduction (27.1)

And Job again took up his parable, and said,

Job's speech is called a "parable" (KJV, ASV). Although many of the later versions have "discourse" (RSV, NASB, NKJV, NIV), "on etymological grounds, the Hebrew term *masal* should mean 'similitude' and many of the *mesalim* (the term applied to the collections in the Book of Proverbs) are pithy comparisons" (AB). The term [S. 4912] is used, especially in Hebrew Wisdom Literature, "of sentences constructed in parallelism" (BDB, 605). The rendering "parable" comes from the Vulgate, and fits the parallelism which runs through the chapter. Such parallelism is characteristic of Hebrew poetry, and some think the word "poem" may be best in this place (AB; *cf.* Ges. 517).

Inflexible Protestation of Innocence (27.2–6)

²As God liveth, who hath taken away my right,
And the Almighty, who hath vexed my soul [Heb. *made my soul bitter*]:
³(For my life is yet whole in me,
And the spirit of God is in my nostrils) [Or, All the while my breath is in me…
    nostrils; surely];
⁴Surely my lips shall [Or, do] not speak unrighteousness,
Neither shall [Or, doth] my tongue utter deceit.
⁵Far be it from me that I should justify you:
Till I die I will not put away mine integrity from me.
⁶My righteousness I hold fast, and will not let it go:
My heart shall not reproach *me* **so long as I live [Or, doth not reproach** *me for*
    any of my days].

Confirmed in their initial suspicions by Job's bold complaints and challenges to God (15.6), the friends are convinced Job must be guilty of great sin, and Eliphaz has even accused him of specific sins (22.5–9). None of Job's arguments or protestations of innocence have had any effect on them. So, with the debate over and the friends having given up the case, Job opens this speech with an oath.

Job swears that he will never yield to the friends' entreaties to confess his sin. He is determined to defend his integrity to the end. He will not permit them to extort a false confession from him. He will never justify the friends by such a false confession of sin. He will defend his righteousness as long as he lives.

Curse Upon His Opponents (27.7–12)

⁷Let mine enemy be as the wicked,
And let him that riseth up against me be as the unrighteous.
⁸For what is the hope of the godless, though he get him gain,
When God taketh away his soul [Or, when God cutteth him off, when he
    taketh *etc.*]?
⁹Will God hear his cry,
When trouble cometh upon him?
¹⁰Will he delight himself in the Almighty,
And call upon God at all times?
¹¹I will teach you concerning the hand of God;
That which is with the Almighty will I not conceal.
¹²Behold, all ye yourselves have seen it;
Why then are ye become altogether vain?

Verse 7 determines the context for the remainder of chapter 27. Job swore that he would never justify the friends by making a deceitful confession of sin. Now he pronounces a curse against any who, like the friends, rise up against him and falsely accuse him: Let such opponents "be as the wicked" (7). This phrase is defined by what follows to the end of the chapter.

Job begins to explain what he means in the description of the godless, who has no hope when God takes away his soul (8), whose cry in time of trouble God will not hear (9), who does not delight in the Almighty and call upon God (10).

Job proposes to teach the three friends "concerning the hand of God" (11). But he is only teaching them what they already know, and, in fact, they have made speech after speech themselves, setting forth what Job now "teaches" them. Job recognizes that they themselves have seen what he is going to teach them about the hand of God as it comes down on sinners (12a). But he has a question for them: "Why then are you become altogether vain?" (12b). The verb [S. 1891] is used here with a cognate accusative, and BDB 211 renders the question: "Why do ye *become vain* with vanity (*i.e.* shew yourselves utterly vain)?" Job is, of course, referring to the speeches of the friends, and Ges. 214 renders: "Why then do ye speak so vainly?"

Job is talking about the wicked, false accusations against him. The friends have talked so much about the terrible fate that comes upon wicked people. They professed to know all about the horrors reserved for the wicked. Yet they have done this wicked deed against him. It seems to Job that they themselves are in need of some teaching about the destiny of the wicked, and he is ready to give them what they need. Let them take warning.

"The Portion of a Wicked Man With God" (27.13–23)

¹³This is the portion of a wicked man with God,
And the heritage of oppressors, which they receive from the Almighty:
¹⁴If his children be multiplied, it is for the sword;
And his offspring shall not be satisfied with bread.
¹⁵Those that remain of him shall be buried in death,
And his widows shall make no lamentation.
¹⁶Though he heap up silver as the dust,
And prepare raiment as the clay;
¹⁷He may prepare it, but the just shall put it on,
And the innocent shall divide the silver.
¹⁸He buildeth his house as the moth,
And as a booth which the keeper maketh.
¹⁹He lieth down rich, but he shall not be gathered *to his fathers*;
He openeth his eyes, and he is not.
²⁰Terrors overtake him like waters;
A tempest stealeth him away in the night.
²¹The east wind carrieth him away, and he departeth;
And it sweepeth him out of his place.
²²For *God* shall hurl at him, and not spare:
He would fain flee out of his hand.
²³Men shall clap their hands at him,
And shall hiss him out of his place.

Job defines what he meant by the curse on his enemy: "Let mine enemy be as the wicked,..." (7). However numerous the offspring of the wicked, they meet with a violent end (14–15). However much wealth he may accumulate, he will not live to enjoy it (16–17). His house will be as flimsy as the moth's cocoon and the booth set up by a keeper of vineyards or gardens (18; *cf.* Isa 1.8; Lam. 2.6). He lies down rich but is not gathered to his fathers (19a), or, as several versions put it, following ancient versions, "but will do so no more" (RSV; NASB and NIV similarly), for his wealth disappears overnight (19b). Terrors come upon him like flood waters (20a). He is swept out of his place as by a storm (20b–22). Men will applaud his desperate plight (23a) and drive him from his place with a hiss of derision (23b).

If Job's description of the destiny of the wicked sounds like the speeches of the friends, and on the surface seems to contradict previous speeches from Job, we must remember that Job does not differ with the friends about the destiny of the wicked. The problem of which he complains is that the wicked often do not seem to suffer as one might expect, but instead prosper, live securely and die a peaceful and honorable death, while he himself suffers the fate one expects a wicked man to experience. His complaint is that God's apparent hostility makes him appear to be a sinner. When Job complains that his afflictions are God's testimony against him (10.17; 16.8), that is tantamount to saying that such afflictions are what one expects sinners to experience. But Job never argues that the righteous always suffer or that the wicked are always prosperous and secure. The problem arises from the exceptions, of which the friends take no note. Their speeches about the justice of God, which invariably reward the righteous and punish the wicked, do not allow for a case like Job's, in which a godly man experiences the afflictions one expects a wicked man to experience.

What makes the present description of the destiny of the wicked seem fitting in Job's mouth is the context, in which he uses this description as an illustration of the curse which Job pronounces on his enemy (7). The friends behaved wickedly against him, and it is they who need the lesson about what happens to wicked persons.

Job has threatened the friends before because of their treatment of him (13.3–12; 19.28–29). Now, in effect, he turns their own speeches about the destiny of the wicked back on them. True, he is teaching them (11f) only what they have been teaching him and, therefore, already knew. But they seem to pay no attention to their own speeches. If they insist on falsely accusing Job, it is they who need the warning about what would happen to a wicked man. Compare Deuteronomy 19.15–21, where the law calls for a false witness to receive the punishment he tries to bring upon another.

This speech is not really in conflict with Job's earlier speeches dwelling upon the prosperity of the wicked. Those earlier speeches grew out of his perplexity over not seeing the wicked receive their just portion from God but, rather, the opposite in many cases. It is this perplexity, growing out of the conflict between what Job expects to see and what he in fact does see, that brings us to the following discourse on wisdom.

Mankind's Failure to Attain Wisdom (28)

The connection of this essay on wisdom with the preceding chapter has been difficult to make out. By rendering the connecting word *Surely*, the various versions confess as much, for *Surely* is not the natural meaning of the Hebrew. "*For* is the natural meaning of the Hebrew word: the text [of the Revised Version] has *surely*, because in the present context of the chapter nothing has preceded, the reason for which can be contained in the verses which now follow" (Driver in ICC, II, 190).

But, as gifted as Driver is at tracing connections of thought, he has certainly missed something in chapter 27 for which chapter 28 provides the explanation. The main thrust of chapter 28, beyond any shadow of a doubt, is the failure of mankind to attain wisdom. It is certainly not difficult to see a connection between that thesis and the charge Job has made against the friends that they *have become altogether vain* (27.12). All that we must do, then, to secure a natural connection between these two chapters is to realize that chapter 28 links into the main thesis of chapter 27 rather than insisting upon a connection with only the last section of chapter 27. What is that main thesis?

As the debate has wound down, and none of the friends arises to answer Job's reply to Bildad (Job 26), Job continues. He begins by asserting his determination to defend his integrity against all the insinuations of his friends. He will not let them badger him into a false confession (27.2–9). Anyone who makes such false accusations against him as the friends have done is an enemy who deserves the portion God has in store for the wicked (7). Job's friends are the ones who need to hear a speech about "the portion of a wicked man with God." So Job resolves to teach the friends about the way God deals with wicked men (11). True, he is only teaching them what they already know, indeed what they have been teaching him. In fact, Job confesses as much: "Behold, all you yourselves have seen it" (12a). But, that being the case, he asks: "Why are you become altogether vain?" (12b). They certainly do not act as though they are afraid of any judgment against the wicked. Their accusations against him have exposed their own emptiness. They are the ones who need to hear about the destiny of the wicked man, and Job gives them back their own sermon in the closing section (13–23). But the sermon on "the portion of a wicked man with God" is not the main point of this speech that comes at the close of the debate. The main point is, rather, Job's determination to defend his integrity against the accusations of the friends and their vanity in the making of these accusations. Chapter 28, then, instead of being linked to the sermon on the destiny of the wicked, with which Job threatens his friends, is connected with the vanity Job has charged against the friends. The connection would then run as follows:

Yes, indeed, you have become altogether vain. And this vanity is no more than a manifestation of the failure of mankind generally to attain to wisdom. Thus chapter 28, coming in as it does at the end of the debate, is Job's judgment on the debate. Job's theologian friends have done their best, but they have not attained wisdom. If the connection I have suggested is correct, and coming as it does from Job, chapter 28 isprimarily Job's judgment about the failure of the friends. But he himself has confessed his own perplexity about his suffering and the failure to see such suffering fall consistently upon those who really deserve it. So Job, no doubt, includes himself among those who have not attained wisdom and understanding. The chapter, therefore, comes in at the close of the debate as an evaluation of the debate as a whole. Human wisdom has done its best, but it has fallen far short of the truth.

Man's Skill at Mining the Treasures of the Earth (28.1–11)

Surely [Or, For] there is a mine for silver,
And a place for gold which they refine.
²Iron is taken out of the earth [Or, dust],
And copper is molten out of the stone.
³*Man* setteth an end to darkness,
And searcheth out, to the furthest bound,
The stones of obscurity and of thick darkness.
⁴He breaketh open a shaft away from where men sojourn;
They are forgotten of the foot;
They hang afar from men [Or, The flood breaketh out from where men
    sojourn; *even the waters* forgotten of the foot: they are diminished, they
    are gone away from man], they swing [Or, flit] to and fro.
⁵As for the earth, out of it cometh bread;

And underneath it is turned up as it were by fire.
⁶The stones thereof are the place of sapphires,
And it hath dust of gold [Or, And he winneth lumps of gold].
⁷That path no bird of prey knoweth,
Neither hath the falcon's eye seen it:
⁸The proud beasts [Heb. *sons of pride*] have not trodden it,
Nor hath the fierce lion passed thereby.
⁹He putteth forth his hand upon the flinty rock;
He overturneth the mountains by the roots.
¹⁰He cutteth out channels [Or, passages] among the rocks;
And his eye seeth every precious thing.
¹¹He bindeth the streams that they trickle not [Heb. *from weeping*];
And the thing that is hid bringeth he forth to light.

The essay on wisdom begins with a description of man's skill at mining the treasures of the earth. The reader is held in suspense, wondering how an essay on mining relates to the subject. Will the writer ever get to the point? At verse 12 he does. The subject is wisdom. How does one get wisdom? For all his skill at finding the treasures of earth, man is extremely limited when it comes to obtaining wisdom.

Wisdom Inaccessible to Man (28.12–22)

¹²But where shall wisdom be found?
And where is the place of understanding?
¹³Man knoweth not the price thereof;
Neither is it found in the land of the living.
¹⁴The deep saith, It is not in me;
And the sea saith, It is not with me.
¹⁵It cannot be gotten for gold [Or, treasure],
Neither shall silver be weighed for the price thereof.
¹⁶It cannot be valued with the gold of Ophir,
With the precious onyx [Or, beryl], or the sapphire.
¹⁷Gold and glass cannot equal it,
Neither shall it be exchanged for jewels [Or, vessels] of fine gold.
¹⁸No mention shall be made of coral or of crystal:
Yea, the price of wisdom is above rubies [Or, red coral; or, pearls].
¹⁹The topaz of Ethiopia shall not equal it,
Neither shall it be valued with pure gold.
²⁰Whence then cometh wisdom?
And where is the place of understanding?

²¹Seeing it is hid from the eyes of all living,
And kept close from the birds of the heavens.
²²Destruction [Heb. *Abaddon*] and Death say,
We have heard a rumor thereof with our ears.

Man has been able to find the precious things of earth. But he is at a loss when it comes to finding wisdom. As valuable and therefore as desirable as wisdom is—the precious metals and jewels of earth cannot be exchanged for it—man has not been able to attain it. But if no price can be set on it and it cannot be purchased with precious metals and jewels, how does one get it? "Whence then comes wisdom?" (20a).

Wisdom the Possession of God Alone (28.23–28)

²³God understandeth the way thereof,
And he knoweth the place thereof.
²⁴For he looketh to the ends of the earth,
And seeth under the whole heaven;
²⁵To make [Or, When he maketh] a weight for the wind:
Yea, he meteth out the waters by measure.
²⁶When he made a decree for the rain,
And a way for the lightning of the thunder;
²⁷Then did he see it, and declare [Or, recount] it;
He established it, yea, and searched it out.
²⁸And unto man he said,
Behold, the fear of the Lord, that is wisdom;
And to depart from evil is understanding.

The concluding verses contain three basic ideas:

First, the assertion that God knows what no man does. He knows where wisdom may be found, for he, in fact, established wisdom when he created the world.

Second, the explanation of why God knows wisdom also clarifies what is meant by wisdom in the thought of the speaker. Wisdom refers to "the intellectual apprehension of the principles by which the course of the physical world and the events of human life are regulated." It involves a grasp of the idea or plan of the world, which lies behind all the phenomena and occurrences of the world and the principles behind the government of the world.

Third, the wisdom that is possible for a man (28). Job himself set forth the portion God has appointed for the wicked (27.13–23). But earlier he expressed perplexity at the failure to observe these principles in operation in many instances (chs 21, 24). This discourse on wisdom concludes that the wisdom behind the operation of the world is beyond the understanding of man. Only the Creator has wisdom in any absolute sense. But he teaches man wisdom by which to live (28). The fear of the Lord is the wisdom that befits the creature. That is sufficient for mankind, and he will have to be content with that, for the rest is beyond his reach.

Coming in, as it does, at the conclusion of the debate, chapter 28 has the effect of a judgment on the debate. Wicked men conclude from the mysteries of divine providence that the fear of God has no special advantages or benefits. What profit should we have, if we pray to him? they ask (*cf.* 21.15). Their own prosperity in their ungodliness seem to be an endorsement of their philosophy. They have not attained to wisdom in any sense.

But Job considers that his friends have become altogether vain as well (27.12). They have done him a wicked injustice by means of their groundless accusations. Thus they have not attained to wisdom.

As for himself, Job can only claim the wisdom God has imparted about the right way to live (28.28). But he is determined to defend his own integrity until the end (*cf.* 27.1–6). His last speech will conclude with his strongest protestation of his innocence (ch 31). But the ways of divine providence remain a mystery beyond his comprehenion. So wisdom has eluded his grasp.

Job's Last Speech (29–31)

Job's last speech is a final, comprehensive survey of his entire mysterious history and cause. It has three parts:

Memory of Past Happiness (Job 29)

And Job again took up his parable, and said,
²Oh that I were as in the months of old,
As in the days when God watched over me;
³When his lamp shined upon [Or, above] my head,
And by his light I walked through darkness;
⁴As I was in the ripeness of my days [Heb. *my days of autumn*],
When the friendship [Or, counsel] of God was upon my tent;
⁵When the Almighty was yet with me,

And my children were about me;

⁶When my steps were washed with butter,

And the rock poured me out streams of oil!

⁷When I went forth to the gate unto the city,

When I prepared my seat in the street [Or, broad place],

⁸The young men saw me and hid themselves,

And the aged rose up and stood;

⁹The princes refrained from talking,

And laid their hand on their mouth;

¹⁰The voice of the nobles was hushed [Heb. *hid*],

And their tongue cleaved to the roof of their mouth.

¹¹For when the ear heard *me*, then it blessed me;

And when the eye saw *me*, it gave witness unto me:

¹²Because I delivered the poor that cried,

The fatherless also, that had none to help him [Or, and him that had *etc*.].

¹³The blessing of him that was ready to perish came upon me;

And I caused the widow's heart to sing for joy.

¹⁴I put on righteousness, and it clothed me [Or, clothed itself with me]:

My justice was as a robe and a diadem [Or, turban].

¹⁵I was eyes to the blind,

And feet was I to the lame.

¹⁶I was a father to the needy:

And the cause of him that I knew not I searched out [Or, the cause which I knew not].

¹⁷And I brake the jaws [Heb. *great teeth*] of the unrighteous,

And plucked the prey out of his teeth.

¹⁸Then I said, I shall die in [Or, beside, Heb. *with*] my nest,

And I shall multiply my days as the sand:

¹⁹My root is spread out [Heb. *opened*] to [Or, by] the waters,

And the dew lieth all night upon my branch;

²⁰My glory is fresh in me,

And my bow is renewed in my hand.

²¹Unto me men gave ear, and waited,

And kept silence for my counsel.

²²After my words they spake not again;

And my speech distilled upon them.

²³And they waited for me as for the rain;

And they opened their mouth wide *as* for the latter rain.

²⁴I smiled on them, when they had no confidence;

And the light of my countenance they cast not down.

²⁵I chose out their way, and sat *as* chief,

And dwelt as a king in the army,
As one that comforteth the mourners.

...a sorrowful, regretful retrospect, including:

1. *The elements of Job's past happiness (2–10),* including the friendship with God, which was the foundation of all (2–6) and the respect in which he was held by all (7–10).

2. *The reason for such respect (11–17).* Such deference as described in 7–10 is commonly manifested toward rich men because of the economic power and political influence exercised by them. But the respect shown Job was grounded on his being a benefactor to so many.

3. *His outlook for the future in those days (18–20).* Job had every expectation of living to a ripe old age, dying a peaceful death at home, and with his reputation and power intact.

4. *Return to the main thought—his high respect and influential place among men (21–25).*

Present Abasement and Humiliation in Contrast to the Former Respect (Job 30)

But now they that are younger than I have me in derision,
Whose fathers I disdained to set with the dogs of my flock.
²Yea, the strength of their hands, whereto should it profit me?
Men in whom ripe age [Or, vigor] is perished.
³They are gaunt with want and famine;
They gnaw the dry ground [Or, They flee into the wilderness, into *etc.*], in
    the gloom [Or, *which* yesternight *was;* Or, on the eve of] of wasteness and
    desolation.
⁴They pluck salt-wort by the bushes;
And the roots of the broom are their food [Or, to warm them].
⁵They are driven forth from the midst *of men;*
They cry after them as after a thief;
⁶So that they dwell in frightful valleys,
In holes of the earth and of the rocks.
⁷Among the bushes they bray;
Under the nettles [Or, wild vetches] they are gathered together [Or, stretch
    themselves].
⁸*They are* children of fools, yea, children of base men [Heb. men of *no name*];
They were scourged out of the land [Or, are outcasts from the land].
⁹And now I am become their song,
Yea, I am a byword unto them.

[10]They abhor me, they stand aloof from me,
And spare not to spit in my face [Or, at the sight of me].
[11]For he hath loosed his cord [Or, According to another reading, *my cord* (or
  bowstring)], and afflicted me;
And they have cast off the bridle before me.
[12]Upon my right hand rise the rabble [Or, brood];
They thrust aside my feet,
And they cast up against me their ways of destruction.
[13]They mar [Or, break up] my path,
They set forward my calamity,
Even men that have no helper.
[14]As through a wide breach they come [Or, As a wide breaking in *of waters*]:
In the midst of the ruin they roll themselves *upon me*.
[15]Terrors are turned upon me;
They chase [Or, Thou chasest] mine honor [Or, my nobility] as the wind;
And my welfare is passed away as a cloud.
[16]And now my soul is poured out within [Heb. *upon*] me;
Days of affliction have taken hold upon me.
[17]In the night season my bones are pierced [Or, corroded *and drop away* from
  me] in [Heb. *from off*] me,
And the *pains* that gnaw me take no rest [Or, my sinews take *etc.*].
[18]By *God's* great force is my garment disfigured;
It bindeth me about as the collar of my coat.
[19]He hath cast me into the mire,
And I am become like dust and ashes.
[20]I cry unto thee, and thou dost not answer me:
I stand up, and thou gazest at me.
[21]Thou art turned to be cruel to me;
With the might of thy hand thou persecutest me.
[22]Thou liftest me up to the wind, thou causest me to ride *upon it*;
And thou dissolvest me in the storm.
[23]For I know that thou wilt bring me to death,
And to the house appointed for all living [Or, the house of meeting for *etc.*].
[24]Howbeit doth not one stretch out the hand in his fall?
Or in his calamity therefore cry for help?
[25]Did not I weep for him that was in trouble?
Was not my soul grieved for the needy?
[26]When I looked for good, then evil came;
And when I waited for light, there came darkness.
[27]My heart is troubled, and resteth not;
Days of affliction are come upon me.

²⁸I go mourning without the sun [Or, blackened, but not by the sun]:
I stand up in the assembly, and cry for help.
²⁹I am a brother to jackals,
And a companion to ostriches.
³⁰My skin is black, *and falleth* from me,
And my bones are burned with heat.
³¹Therefore is my harp *turned* to mourning,
And my pipe into the voice of them that weep.

1. The low class of men who now hold Job in contempt (1–8). Job had been reverenced by the young and the old, even princes and nobles (29.7–10). But now he is treated with contempt by those who are themselves contemptible, social outcasts who live like animals away from the society of respectable people.

2. Job's present contemptuous treatment at the hands of such outcasts (9–15). Job's former condition had been a restraint upon such treatment, but now the bridle is off (11). Take note of the imagery in which Job is compared to a city under siege (12ff).

3. Description of the miserable condition to which Job has been reduced (16–23). Some description of his miserable state (16–19) is followed by God's unresponsiveness to his outcry (20). Observe the direct address to God (20–23). Job no longer enjoys the close friendship with God described at the beginning (29.2–6), but he feels that God has become cruel toward him, persecuting him with almighty power (21). Job is like one caught up in a destructive storm (22). He knows God will bring him to death and the house where all the living eventually meet (23).

4. A final contrast between the compassion he had formerly shown others and his own mournful and unpitied state in the present (24–31). One naturally stretches out his hand and cries for help when he is in trouble (24). Job himself had responded to such cries, showing sympathy toward one in trouble (25). His life being as it was, he had looked for good (*cf.* 29.18–20), but, contrary to expectation, he received bad things instead (26). With troubled heart, amidst days of affliction (27), he stands up in the assembly and cries for help (28), but his cry goes unanswered, and he feels akin to the howling jackals or screeching ostriches of the desert (29). In his misery (30), the music of his former life has been changed into mourning (31).

Solemn Declaration of Innocence (31.1–34)

I made a covenant with mine eyes;
How then should I look upon a virgin?
²For what is the portion from God above,
And the heritage from the Almighty on high? [Or, For what portion should I
    have of God… and what heritage *etc.*? Is there not calamity *etc.*?]
³Is it not calamity to the unrighteous,
And disaster to the workers of iniquity?
⁴Doth not he see my ways,
And number all my steps?
⁵If I have walked with falsehood,
And my foot hath hasted to deceit
⁶(Let me be weighed in an even balance,
That God may know mine integrity);
⁷If my step hath turned out of the way,
And my heart walked after mine eyes,
And if any spot hath cleaved to my hands:
⁸Then let me sow, and let another eat;
Yea, let the produce [Or, my offspring, Heb. *my produce*] of my field be
    rooted out.
⁹If my heart hath been enticed unto a woman,
And I have laid wait at my neighbor's door;
¹⁰Then let my wife grind unto another,
And let others bow down upon her.
¹¹For that were a heinous crime;
Yea, it were an iniquity to be punished by the judges:
¹²For it is a fire that consumeth unto Destruction [Heb. *Abaddon*. See 26.6],
And would root out all mine increase.
¹³If I have despised the cause of my man-servant or of my maid-servant,
When they contended with me;
¹⁴What then shall I do when God riseth up?
And when he visiteth, what shall I answer him?
¹⁵Did not he that made me in the womb make him?
And did not one fashion us in the womb?
¹⁶If I have withheld the poor from *their* desire [Or, aught that the poor
    desired],
Or have caused the eyes of the widow to fail,
¹⁷Or have eaten my morsel alone,
And the fatherless hath not eaten thereof;
¹⁸(Nay, from my youth he grew up with me as with a father,
And her have I guided from my mother's womb);

¹⁹If I have seen any perish for want of clothing,
Or that the needy had no covering;
²⁰If his loins have not blessed me,
And if he hath not been warmed with the fleece of my sheep;
²¹If I have lifted up my hand against the fatherless,
Because I saw my help in the gate:
²²Then let my shoulder fall from the shoulder-blade,
And mine arm be broken from the bone.
²³For calamity from God is a terror to me,
And by reason of his majesty I can do nothing.
²⁴If I have made gold my hope,
And have said to the fine gold, *Thou art* my confidence;
²⁵If I have rejoiced because my wealth was great,
And because my hand had gotten much;
²⁶If I have beheld the sun [Heb. *the light*] when it shined,
Or the moon walking in brightness,
²⁷And my heart hath been secretly enticed,
And my mouth hath kissed my hand [Heb. *my hand hath kissed my mouth*]:
²⁸This also were an iniquity to be punished by the judges;
For I should have denied the God that is above.
²⁹If I have rejoiced at the destruction of him that hated me,
Or lifted up myself when evil found him;
³⁰(Yea, I have not suffered my mouth [Heb. *palate*] to sin
By asking his life with a curse);
³¹If the men of my tent have not said,
Who can find one that hath not been filled with his meat?
³²(The sojourner hath not lodged in the street;
But I have opened my doors to the traveller [Heb. *the way*]);
³³If like Adam [Or, after the manner of men] I have covered my
    transgressions,
By hiding mine iniquity in my bosom,
³⁴Because I feared the great multitude,
And the contempt of families terrified me,
So that I kept silence, and went not out of the door—

Whatever the appearances, Job goes on record that the reversal that has taken place in his circumstances cannot be justified by sin found in himself. At several points Job's repudiation of guilt takes the form of an oath, bringing upon himself a curse if he is not innocent of the sin he denies. What else can he do? He has been directly accused of wrongdoing by the friends. The afflictions he has suffered have lent plausibility to the charges, according to the traditional theory. He cannot prove his innocence. He can only swear to it in the sight of God and assert with boldness that he has nothing to fear from any charge against him. Job claims to be:

1. Not guilty of lust (1–4).
2. Not guilty of dishonesty (5–8).
3. Not guilty of adultery (9–12).
4. Not guilty of abuse of power (13–23), including:
    4a. Mistreatment of servants (13–15).
    4b. Hardness of heart toward the poor and needy (16–20).
    4c. Perversion of justice in court against the defenseless (21–23).
5. Not guilty of idolatry (24–28), including two forms.
6. Not guilty of vindictiveness (29–30).
7. Not guilty of stinginess (31–32).
8. Not guilty of hypocrisy (33–34).
9. See below, after 35–37.

Climactic Final Plea That His Case Be Heard (31.35–37)

³⁵Oh that I had one to hear me!
(Lo, here is my signature [Heb. *mark*], let the Almighty answer me);
And *that I had* the indictment [Heb. *book*] which mine adversary hath written!
³⁶Surely I would carry it upon my shoulder;
I would bind it unto me as a crown:
³⁷I would declare unto him the number of my steps;
As a prince would I go near unto him.

An outburst! The language relates to court practices. Job has repeatedly pleaded for an opportunity to appear before God and argue his case. Now, finally, near the close of his protestation of innocence, as almost his last words, he pleads once again: "Oh that I had one to hear me!" (35a). In effect, as the defendant in the case, he signs his mark (*i.e.* signature) to his protestation of innocence. He signs his name to his claim of innocence and pleads for an answer from God (35b). He wishes to see the book written by his opponent—*i.e.*, the book with the charges against him (35c; *cf.* 13.26). Verses 36f are a strong insistence that this book could contain nothing of which he need be ashamed. Instead of trying to hide it, he would carry it on his shoulder and wear it as a king might wear a crown. He would be willing to have his life examined (37a). He would approach God with the dignity of a prince (37b)—not as a criminal who fears coming before his judge.

It may seem incongruous that this outburst comes in before the protestation of innocence is complete. Job still has one more "not guilty" plea to make. Should these verses not stand at the very end? I think such strict logic and order is too much to expect from a man who has been building up a head of emotional "steam." Job can restrain himself no longer. The passage is indeed "an outburst" of pent-up emotion.

9. Not Guilty of Exploitation (31.38–40)

³⁸If my land crieth out against me,
And the furrows thereof weep together;
³⁹If I have eaten the fruits [Heb. *strength*] thereof without money,
Or have caused the owners thereof to lose their life:
⁴⁰Let thistles [Or, thorns] grow instead of wheat,
And cockle [Or, noisome weeds] instead of barley.
The words of Job are ended.

Evaluation: How Matters Stand at the Close of the Debate

In a sense, Job has won the debate. He has silenced the friends, who despair of convicting Job of sin, however convinced they are that he is guilty. So they do not continue the debate (32.1).

But Job has argued his own innocence ("justified himself") at the cost of leaving God in an extremely bad light—*i.e.*, putting God in the wrong, accusing God of perversion of justice (*cf.* 32.2).

The case cannot be left as it is. Job must be answered. The resolution of the problem comes in two stages, and, as we shall see, two stages are necessary. First a younger man arises to provide a review of the debate. Then Jehovah himself speaks and puts Job in his place. Job has to be put in his place. But it has to be done in a way that does not leave him feeling mistreated, having simply been silenced by superior power. He must not be left feeling that he has been wronged but, rather, satisfied that he has been dealt with fairly. Only then can he be left with a faith in God that is altogether what it ought to be. This is the argument for the necessity of two stages in the resolution.

Resolution

Job 32–42

Introduction to the Two Part Resolution of the Problem

We come now to the resolution of the issues raised in the book of Job. The resolution comes in two parts, and both are necessary. The last part of the book is the revelation of Jehovah, and this self-revelation certainly accomplishes a necessary purpose. But some seem to assume that Jehovah's self-revelation is all that is necessary, and I believe that view needs to be challenged. The speeches of Elihu serve an equally necessary purpose, and the book would not be the same without them. Before delving into the exposition of the the text, I must offer some introductory suggestions about the role of Elihu and the role of Jehovah in an attempt to clarify the part each plays.

The State of the Case at the End of the Debate

The experiment proposed by Satan in the prologue did not have the predicted results (1.9–12; 2.4–5). Satan cast doubt upon the genuineness of Job's piety, suggesting that Job only served God for selfish reasons and not out of pure devotion to God, predicting that Job would turn his back on God once all material rewards were taken away. The afflictions, therefore, were proposed as a test of Job's piety.

As matters stand at the end of the debate Job has proved Satan a liar and a slanderer. Despite the severe trials, he has not renounced God but has clung to God to the end. However, the results of the experiment have not been totally positive, for—under the influence of the traditional theology defended by his friends, which sees an absolute cause and effect relationship between sin and suffering—Job has been driven to make ungodly accusations against God. Although Job's faith has held out, certain weaknesses or defects have been brought to light by the trial. His faith has need of correction and purification. The two remaining portions of the book supply what is lacking.

Job's last speech closes with a final plea that his case might be heard (31.35–37). He feels God has done him wrong, treating him as a sinner when in fact he is innocent of any wrongdoing which would justify the afflictions he is suffering. But, when such appeals were made previously, two contrasting scenarios were imagined. On the one hand, Job feared that God would bring his infinite power and wisdom to bear against him, so that he would not be able to make out his case even if granted the opportunity (9.1–20, 28–35; 13.3, 13–28; 23.13–17). On the other, he had imagined that he might be able to come before God and to reason with him, without being intimidated by the greatness of God's power (23.3–7).

The fact is, Job's final demand to be heard and the confidence he expresses about the boldness with which he would approach God if he did have the opportunity to be heard are characterized by pure, unmitigated, outrageous arrogance. Job certainly needs to be brought to his knees before the Almighty.

Jehovah's Self-Revelation

That is, in fact, exactly what happens when Jehovah manifests himself to Job (chs 38–42.6). The Almighty does eventually answer Job, but not as Job wishes, rather as he fears. When Jehovah does reveal himself to Job he does not examine Job's plea of innocence. He does not explain Job's suffering. He does not defend his providence. He does not answer Job's questions. The Almighty does not have to explain himself or to give an account to puny human beings. Job was certainly right about that (9.12, 19).

Job had feared that, even if he had a chance to argue his case before the Almighty, he would be overwhelmed by infinite power and not have a fair chance to present his case; in effect, that he would be bullied into silence (B. S. Childs). In fact, when the time comes, Job is humbled by the overwhelming power and majesty of the Almighty; he makes no attempt to argue a case. But what else could one expect? Could one really expect successfully to argue with God? Job receives from God the one thing his complaints demanded. He is put in his proper place before the Almighty.

Elihu

Yet Job will not feel he has been forced into submission against his will nor bullied into silence. He will not feel the resentment of one forced into submission by superior power; he will not feel that he had a just cause to maintain which has not been considered. What, we must ask, will satisfy the mind of Job and cause him to feel contentment rather than resentment? The answer is Elihu, who enters the proceedings ahead of Jehovah and prepares Job's mind for the revelation of Jehovah. Elihu speaks not as one of infinite power and wisdom who would overwhelm Job with divine majesty, but one "formed out of the clay" just like Job, an equal who would be able to answer Job's complaints and to set his mind at rest. Job needs to be put in his place all right, but he also needs to have his mind satisfied. He needs explanations that will put his arguments and complaints to rest. That is the accomplishment of Elihu, who comes in as a forerunner of Jehovah, preparing the way for Jehovah and introducing him.

Elihu gives a review and evaluation of the debate between Job and his friends. He recognizes that the friends have not answered Job's arguments and complaints. Yet they begged to be answered. Job has been falsely accused by the friends. They were not able to vindicate God without accusing Job. But Job himself has not been able to defend his own integrity without slandering the Almighty, and his complaints cannot be allowed to stand. He has to be answered, and the answer has to be grounded in reason and truth. It cannot be an answer imposed by overwhelming power. It has to be an answer that Job's mind can understand and accept.

Elihu does what the friends failed to do. He challenges and rebukes Job for his blasphemous accusations against God. He refutes and corrects Job's false thinking about God, especially the view that God is acting as an enemy toward him. But he answers Job not by attacking Job, but by explaining and defending God; *i.e.*, by helping Job to understand God. (Incidentally, he accomplishes his task without assuming on the ground of Job's suffering that he must be a wicked man.) In that way, he prepares Job's heart for the speeches of Jehovah, which will bring Job to his knees and put him in his proper place before God.

Elihu provides answers to Job's complaints and does not just outtalk Job. He gives Job ample opportunity to respond (33.1–7, 31–33). The fiesty Job had responded to each of the friends and defeated them in debate. As long as one of them wanted to speak, Job was ready with an answer. But he does not answer Elihu. Evidently Elihu's reasoning satisfies Job's mind.

When Jehovah at length reveals himself with overwhelming majesty, Job finds himself no match for him, but he can accept his position in relation to God without resentment and be at rest.

The Book of Job Self-Correcting

The view that Elihu contributes nothing to the thought of the Book of Job is more than improbable; it is impossible. The book is self-correcting. That is the fundamental premise on which I have proceeded from the beginning. Job answers the friends, and Elihu answers Job. But no one answers Elihu. Job does not answer him, though he has the chance. Nor does Jehovah, who is critical of both Job and the friends. Evidently the author of this book sees Elihu as playing an essential role, introducing the revelation of Jehovah at the end.

It is more than strange to me that so many commentators take it upon themselves to explain what is wrong with Elihu, when the Book of Job itself finds no fault with him. The author evidently considers Elihu to represent the first stage in the resolution of the great problem that has been debated in this book. I consider the book sufficient in itself and, therefore, will take the view of the author. I will not undertake to rewrite it and to supply the answer to Elihu which the author omitted. I do not believe Elihu needs to be answered. Nor did the author.

Now we are ready to examine the text.

Speeches of Elihu, Preparing the Way for the Revelation of Jehovah (Job 32–37)

Introduction of Elihu and Explanation of his Reasons for Speaking (32)

Introductory Narrative Explaining the Circumstances in which Elihu Felt Compelled to Speak (32.1–5)

So these three men ceased to answer Job, because he was righteous in his own eyes. ²Then was kindled the wrath of Elihu the son of Barachel the Buzite, of the family of Ram: against Job was his wrath kindled, because he justified himself rather than God. ³Also against his three friends was his wrath kindled, because they had found no answer, and yet had condemned Job.

⁴Now Elihu had waited to speak unto Job [Heb. *waited for Job with words*], because they were elder than he. ⁵And when Elihu saw that there was no answer in the mouth of these three men, his wrath was kindled.

The friends quit the debate because they were unable to convict Job of sin (1). Elihu, a younger man, had held back out of deference to his elders (4). But he has listened to the debate and is hot with anger at its close.

First he is angry with Job because he put himself in the right rather than God (2). Given the traditional view with regard to the absolute and invariable connection between sin and suffering, Job saw no way to defend his own innocence without accusing God of injustice. He charged God with perversion of justice in his case.

Then Elihu is angry at the friends because they have not been able to answer Job's charges against God and, thus, to condemn him or prove him wrong (3, *cf.* NEB margin).

Rationale of Elihu's Speeches Founded on the Failure of the Friends (32.6–22)

Explanation: Why Elihu Held Back Before But Speaks Now (32.6–10)

⁶And Elihu the son of Barachel the Buzite answered and said,
I am young, and ye are very old;
Wherefore I held back, and durst not show you mine opinion.
⁷I said, Days should speak,
And multitude of years should teach wisdom.
⁸But there is a spirit in man,
And the breath of the Almighty giveth them understanding.
⁹It is not the great that are wise,
Nor the aged that understand justice.
¹⁰Therefore I said [Or, say], Hearken to me;
I also will show mine opinion.

Elihu explains that he refrained from speaking before out of respect to the age of the friends (6f), but then sets forth his own claim to wisdom and understanding as a divine creation, divinely gifted (8; *cf.* Gen 2.7). Wisdom and understanding are gifts of God—not the sole prerogative of age (10).

Further Explanation of Elihu's Speeches: The Failure of the Friends to Answer Job (32.11–14)

¹¹Behold, I waited for your words,
I listened for your reasonings,
Whilst ye searched out what to say.
¹²Yea, I attended unto you,
And, behold, there was none that convinced Job,
Or that answered his words, among you.
¹³Beware lest ye say, We have found wisdom;
God may vanquish him, not man: [Or, Lest ye should say, We have found out
    wisdom; God thrusteth him down, not man; now he *etc.*]
¹⁴For he hath not directed his words against me;
Neither will I answer him with your speeches.

Elihu paid careful attention to the friends' speeches and observed their failure to answer Job (11f). He will not permit them to claim that they have discovered the part of wisdom he has not. To do so would to be to give up the discussion and leave Job to God, since man cannot handle him (13; *cf.* Amos 5.13). For Job has not dealt with Elihu yet (14).

This last verse has particular importance as it indicates Elihu's claim to be taking a position distinct from that of the friends. Many scholars hold that Elihu presents nothing which is not already found in the friends. But Elihu claims from the outset that his position is different from theirs. So we must follow his reasoning carefully to see if he makes good his claim.

The Compelling Necessity Elihu Feels (32.15–22)

¹⁵They are amazed, they answer no more:
They have not a word to say.
¹⁶And shall I wait, because they speak not,
Because they stand still, and answer no more?
¹⁷I also will answer my part,
I also will show mine opinion.
¹⁸For I am full of words;
The spirit within me constraineth me.
¹⁹Behold, my breast is as wine which hath no vent;
Like new wine-skins it is ready to burst [Or, which are ready].
²⁰I will speak, that I may be refreshed [Or, find relief];
I will open my lips and answer.
²¹Let me not, I pray you, respect any man's person;

Neither will I give flattering titles unto any man.
²²For I know not to give flattering titles;
Else would my Maker soon take me away.

Since the failure of the friends is manifest—clearly they have no more to say—Elihu resolves to speak (15–17), and he has good reason: Whereas "they have not a word to say" (15b), he is so "full of words" he is about to burst and must speak in order to relieve this pressure (18–20). Furthermore, he is determined to speak "without fear or favor" (21–22). The friends need not expect flattery or compliments.

First Answer to Job: God Not Job's Enemy (33)

Challenge to Prepare for Controversy (33.1–7)

Howbeit, Job, I pray thee, hear my speech,
And hearken to all my words.
²Behold now, I have opened my mouth;
My tongue hath spoken in my mouth [Heb. *palate*].
³My words *shall utter* the uprightness of my heart;
And that which my lips know they shall speak sincerely.
⁴The Spirit of God hath made me,
And the breath of the Almighty giveth me life.
⁵If thou canst, answer thou me;
Set *thy words* in order before me, stand forth.
⁶Behold, I am toward God even as thou art [Or, I am according to thy wish in God's stead]:
I also am formed out of the clay.
⁷Behold, my terror shall not make thee afraid,
Neither shall my pressure be heavy upon thee.

Elihu turns to Job with an appeal for his attention (1–2). He promises to speak sincerely (3). He speaks in the capacity of a man, a divine creation (4). He challenges Job to prepare his arguments and answer if he can (5). Since he is a lowly creature of God as Job is (6), Job should not feel intimidated by superior force (7).

Verse 7 alludes to Job's complaint that the majesty and power of God is so great that he knew he would be so overawed and overwhelmed in the presence of God that he would not have a fair chance to plead his cause and establish his claim (ch 9, esp. verses 2–3, 13–20, 32–35; 13.20–22).

This passage has special importance in defining the role of Elihu. Observe especially Job's remark that man "cannot answer him one of a thousand" (9.3). In fact, that is exactly Job's situation when Jehovah manifests himself (40.3–5; *cf.* 42.1–6). Job is simply overwhelmed. He is totally unable to contend with God.

Now consider: Without Elihu, Jehovah's intimidating majesty would have silenced Job, but it would not have satisfied his heart and given him peace. He likely would have felt that he had a case to make, but no fair chance to make it. He would have been forced into submission without having the answers and the explanations necessary to understanding God's position.

Only a man like himself can meet him on equal terms and discuss matters with Job in terms that will leave Job feeling satisfied at the end that he had has a fair opportunity to make good his case, and he simply cannot do it. In that way Elihu serves as the "umpire" between Job and God, which Job had felt so necessary to the case (9.32f). Elihu's reproof works conviction in Job's heart. When Jehovah enters the picture, this necessary work has already been accomplished in Job's heart, and Job can submit to Jehovah's overwhelming superiority without any feelings of resentment whatever.

The Issue Drawn: Job's Complaint Against God (33.8–12)

⁸Surely thou hast spoken in my hearing,
And I have heard the voice of *thy* words, *saying,*
⁹I am clean, without transgression;
I am innocent, neither is there iniquity in me:
¹⁰Behold, he findeth occasions [Or, causes of alienation] against me,
He counteth me for his enemy:
¹¹He putteth my feet in the stocks,
He marketh all my paths.
¹²Behold, I will answer thee, in this thou art not just [Or, in this thou art not
**   just: I will answer thee; for *etc.*];**
For God is greater than man.

Elihu cites Job's own words—sometimes verbatim, but sometimes only a summary of the substance. Job claimed to be innocent (9; *cf.* 9.21; 10.7; 12.4; 13.18, 23; 16.17; 23.10–12; 27.5; 29.11–17; ch 31). Yet the traditional view of sin and suffering convinced him that God is treating him as a sinner. So God has no case against him, and Job charged him with making one up, trying to find some occasion for picking a quarrel with him, treating him as an enemy, putting his feet in the stocks, *etc.* (10–11; *cf.* 10.5–7, 13–17; 13.23–27; 19.6–12).

Here is where Elihu draws the issue (12). Probably verse 12 should be read as NKJV (similarly in ASV margin): "Look, in this you are not righteous. I will answer you. For God is greater than man." The verse offers a reason why Elihu and not God himself answers Job. God does not stoop to argue with a man or to defend himself. Therefore, Elihu answers in his behalf.

Refutation of Job's Position (33.13–28)

¹³Why dost thou strive against him,
For that he giveth not account of any of his matters?
¹⁴For God speaketh once [Or, in one way, yea, in two],
Yea twice, *though man* regardeth it not.
¹⁵In a dream, in a vision of the night,
When deep sleep falleth upon men,
In slumberings upon the bed;
¹⁶Then he openeth [Heb. *uncovereth*] the ears of men,
And sealeth their instruction,
¹⁷That he may withdraw man *from his* purpose,
And hide pride from man [Or, That man may put away his purpose, and that
     he may hide];
¹⁸ [Or, That he may keep back] He keepeth back his soul from the pit,
And his life from perishing by the sword [Or, weapons].
And with continual strife in his bones
¹⁹He is chastened also with pain upon his bed,
[Another reading is, While all his bones are firm];
²⁰So that his life abhorreth bread,
And his soul dainty food.
²¹His flesh is consumed away, that it cannot be seen;
And his bones that were not seen stick out.
²²Yea, his soul draweth near unto the pit,
And his life to the destroyers.
²³If there be with him an angel [Or, a messenger],
An interpreter, one among a thousand [Or, of the thousand],
To show unto man what is right for him [Or, his uprightness];
²⁴Then *God* is gracious unto him, and saith,
Deliver him from going down to the pit,
I have found a ransom. [Or, And he be gracious... and say... ransom: his
     flesh *etc.*]

²⁵His flesh shall be fresher than a child's;
He returneth to the days of his youth.
²⁶He prayeth unto God, and he is favorable unto him,
So that he seeth his face with joy:
And he restoreth unto man his righteousness.
²⁷He singeth before men [Or, looketh upon men], and saith,
I have sinned, and perverted that which was right,
And it profited me not [Or, it was not requited unto me, Or, it was not meet
    for me]:
²⁸He hath redeemed my soul from going into the pit,
And my life shall behold the light.

Job complained that God had treated him unfairly. Despite Job's innocence, God treated him as an enemy, locking his feet in stocks, and he would not explain the reason for his actions (13; *cf.* 13.23f; 19.7; 23.1–9; 30.20).

Elihu denies it. God does speak, in fact, in more ways than one, though man often disregards it (14):

1. *Dreams (15–18).* God speaks in dreams for the purpose of opening the ears of men and turning them aside from some evil and destructive course of action (*cf.* Gen 20.3 for an example).

2. *Affliction (19–28).* God also uses sickness and pain, presumably when other measures have failed, to chasten and correct, man—sometimes being brought right to death's door (19–22; *cf.* Gen 12.17). God may use an angel (= messenger, perhaps a human messenger like Elihu himself) in connection with such suffering as an "interpreter," helping the sufferer to understand the meaning of his experience and the direction God wants him to take (23). When the sufferer has learned the right way, then God shows his favor toward him and orders his deliverance from death, announcing that he has found a ransom enabling this person to be delivered (24). Several consequences follow: physical recovery (25), restoration of joyous fellowship with God and vindication of spiritual status (26), confession of sin and praise for deliverance (27–28).

Concluding Summary and Appeal to Job (33.29–33)

²⁹Lo, all these things doth God work,
Twice, *yea* thrice, with a man,
³⁰To bring back his soul from the pit,
That he may be enlightened with the light of the living [Or, life].

³¹Mark well, O Job, hearken unto me:
Hold thy peace, and I will speak.
³²If thou hast anything to say, answer me:
Speak, for I desire to justify thee.
³³If not, hearken thou unto me:
Hold thy peace, and I will teach thee wisdom.

Elihu summarizes with the remark that God works all these things to rescue a man from death and enlighten him with the light of life (29–30).

Thus God may even use affliction for merciful purposes. Job's afflictions, therefore, need not be seen as a sign that God has turned against him (8–11), or as a punishment for sin. For God uses such experiences with merciful intent, as a means of instruction, working out his good purposes in human lives.

The section closes with a direct appeal to Job (31–33), who is given an opportunity to answer Elihu if he can (*cf.* 5). Elihu tells Job: "I desire to justify you" (32b). He had charged that Job was not in the right when he complained against God the way he had (12). But Elihu is not out to condemn Job as a sinner. He wants to help him overcome his problem with God and to come to the right position. He is certainly providing Job with ample reason to speak out if he has anything to say. If, on the other hand, Job has nothing to say, then he is invited to continue to listen and learn wisdom from Elihu (33).

Job does not answer, and Elihu continues. Apparently the author represents Job as seeing something in Elihu that he had not seen in the friends. Elihu's reproof is beginning to take hold; it is producing conviction in Job, whose heart is beginning to soften.

Addendum: Elihu and the Friends

Elihu had recognized the failure of the friends to answer Job, and claimed: "I will not answer him with your speeches" (32:14b). Yet many good scholars have failed to detect a substantive difference between Elihu and the friends. Basically they think Elihu has answered Job with the friends' speeches and has contributed little or nothing toward the solution to the problem. Let me be plain, because such views fail to recognize the major part played by Elihu in the resolution of the problem discussed in the debate. The book could not be brought to a satisfactory solution without Elihu, and that is the author's own view of the matter.

We must insist that this book is self-correcting. We do not need commentators to tell us what is wrong with the reasoning of each speaker. The book corrects itself. Job answers the friends. Elihu answers Job. But no one answers Elihu. He quite obviously takes a point of view which is advocated by the author of the book as a whole. And this book of inspired scripture is sufficient in itself. It does not need to be rewritten to correct a few flaws which would not be detected without the wisdom of the commentators.

We must start by tracing the development of the friends' stand with regard to Job. The debate starts with Job's complaint (in ch 3). Eliphaz makes a friendly enough beginning, even expressing confidence in Job's piety (4.1–11). But he warns Job about criticizing divine providence and implying that man is more righteous than God (4.17 in context of 12–21). He warns Job about "vexation"— bitter resentment of treatment one regards as unjust (5.1–7). He exhorts Job to seek after God (5.8–16) and to submit to correction and chastisement (5.17–27), which explains his view of Job's suffering.

That is a pretty reasonable beginning. But when Job defends his outburst and continues to complain of unjust treatment from God and of the moral indifference with which the world seems to be governed, the harshness of the friends' speeches increases. Zophar's unsympathetic judgment that Job is suffering less than his iniquity deserves (11.1–6) comes in response to Job's complaints. He is not just trying to be mean. He thinks Job's complaints give evidence that he is a very great sinner.

But that sort of response just outrages Job even more, and his honest complaints with regard to divine providence are met by a series of warnings in the second round of speeches about the destiny of wicked men. By the third round of speeches Eliphaz concludes that Job is suffering because of the greatness of his wickedness and even thinks he can identify the sins of which Job is probably guilty (22.1–11).

Elihu's purpose is not to establish the reason Job is suffering, or to argue that Job is a wicked man, but to reprove Job for the ungodly complaints he has made against God and to vindicate God. He does not assume that Job is suffering because he is a great sinner. He wants to help Job understand his suffering from a different point of view, to take away Job's complaints and heal his troubled mind, thus putting him in the right. "I desire to justify you," he says (33.32). His discussion of affliction is in a different context. His charges against Job relate solely to Job's speeches, which have been spoken in his hearing (8). His purpose is to answer Job's complaint that God is groundlessly treating him as an enemy and will not answer his inquiries into the reason. His reply is twofold: (1) God does speak in many ways. One is in dreams, but another is through affliction and pain. (2) Even in affliction, God is not treating him as an enemy, but rather using affliction for a merciful purpose. Job's complaint is, therefore, altogether groundless.

Certainly by the end of the debate none of the three friends could or would have denied that God acted with hostility toward Job. To the contrary, they thought he was, and with good reason. But Elihu does deny that God regards Job as an enemy and argues, rather, that God is being a friend to Job, reasoning that even affliction arises from kindly and merciful purpose on God's part.

But does his discussion of affliction not imply that there is sin or imperfection in the sufferer? Perhaps so. He especially mentions pride as a sin from which God wants to keep man (33.17). But Job has not denied that he has sin in his life; he only denies that he is a wicked man deserving of the afflictions he suffers. He mentions the sins of his youth (13.26). He speaks of the general uncleanness of mankind (14.4 with 25.4). When he wonders, even on the assumption that he has sinned, why God does not pardon his transgression (8.21), he does so not as a man who thinks sin is only a small thing which ought to be overlooked by God, but as a man who has always sought God's forgiveness for his sins (*cf.* 1.5). So Job has not claimed to be a sinless man, but only that he is not the wicked man his sufferings have made him appear to be. I argued in the introduction to Elihu that, although Job has not turned his back on God, the trial has exposed imperfections in Job. Elihu seems to argue that the trial being endured by Job is a refining process aimed at making him an even better man. The friends see Job as a wicked man, but Elihu does not.

He does, however, see him as being guilty of grievous sin in his complaints against God. Job made charges against God such as one might expect from a wicked man (34.1–9), and Elihu feels confident that men of understanding would judge Job's words to be without wisdom; that he is "answering like wicked men" (34.34–37). But who can deny it?

In my opinion, many commentators feel so much sympathy for Job because of his suffering, both physical and psychological, that they try to soften his words. They show a respect of persons toward Job, which has keeps from understanding Elihu. True, Job's blasphemous words arise from mitigating circumstances. We can certainly understand the circumstances. But he does say them, and they are wicked words; and Job sorely needs to repent.

In his complaints against God Job is certainly not just (33.12). But Elihu wants to justify Job (33.32)—*i.e.*, to put him altogether in the right. To that end he endeavors to help Job see affliction in a different light, and to understand the wickedness of his words against God. He deals with the first point in chapter 33 and turns to the second in chapter 34 and, I believe, successfully. He touches Job's heart with his reasoning, and that is why Job has no answer.

Second Answer to Job: The Verdict of Wise Men on the Words of Job (34)

Job does not take advantage of the opportunity to respond to Elihu. So Elihu continues.

Wise Men Challenged to Determine Right (34.1–4)

Moreover Elihu answered and said,
²Hear my words, ye wise men;
And give ear unto me, ye that have knowledge.
³For the ear trieth words,
As the palate tasteth food.
⁴Let us choose for us that which is right:
Let us know among ourselves what is good.

The address is not specifically to the three friends, who have already been discredited (32.9, 11–14), but to whatever "wise men" (2) may be present, calling upon them to consider Elihu's words. Mankind has a faculty for testing words just as for tasting food (3). Wise men are, therefore, challenged to use their faculties for testing words and to determine and choose what is right (4; *cf.* 1 Thess 5.21f).

The Reason for the Challenge: Job's Blasphemous Accusations Against God (34.5–9)

⁵For Job hath said, I am righteous,
And God hath taken away my right:
⁶Notwithstanding my right I am *accounted* a liar [Or, Should I lie against my right?];

My wound [Heb. *Mine arrow*] is incurable, *though I am* without transgression.
⁷What man is like Job,
Who drinketh up scoffing like water,
⁸Who goeth in company with the workers of iniquity,
And walketh with wicked men?
⁹For he hath said, It profiteth a man nothing
That he should delight himself with God [Or, consent with. See Psa 50.18].

Elihu challenges wise men to test and evaluate Job's blasphemous language. Job's position is partly quoted verbatim (5a with 13.18, 5b with 27.2), partly summarized in essence (9.15, 20f; 10.7a; 23.10; 27.6f). He claimed to be righteous and complained that God had taken away his right as an innocent man, treating him as if he were guilty (5). He was in the right, but his treatment by God made all his protestations of innocence seem to be a lie (6a). For the reference to arrows wounding him (6b), consult 6.4.

The question (7f) implies that Job's equal is not to be found for imbibing the scoffing words of the wicked. The words cited in verse 9 most nearly resemble the philosophy of the wicked cited by Job (21.15) and then Eliphaz (22.17), but Job's references to the prosperity of the wicked (esp. 21.7–16) certainly justify Elihu's attributing them to Job.

It should be noted that Elihu's charges relate to Job's speeches. He does not argue that Job's suffering is a punishment for past sins. Verse 9 proves that Elihu is thinking of Job's speeches when he says Job is walking with wicked men (8).

Refutation Addressed to Men of Understanding: The Foundation Principle for Dealing with Such Problems as Job's (34.10–15)

¹⁰Therefore hearken unto me, ye men of understanding:
Far be it from God, that he should do wickedness,
And from the Almighty, that he should commit iniquity.
¹¹For the work of a man will he render unto him,
And cause every man to find according to his ways.
¹²Yea, of a surety, God will not do wickedly,
Neither will the Almighty pervert justice.
¹³Who gave him [Or, laid upon him] a charge over the earth? Or who hath
    disposed the whole world?
¹⁴If he set his heart upon himself [Or, man; Heb. *him*] [Or, According to
    another reading, If he cause his heart to return unto himself]

If he gather unto himself his spirit and his breath;
¹⁵All flesh shall perish together,
And man shall turn again unto dust.

In dealing with such thorny problems as the case of Job presents, one must start with what he knows for sure as an unshakeable foundation. Job asserted that God had done him wrong (5f). But whatever the uncertainties posed by Job's mysterious case, the one thing known for sure is that "the Judge of all the earth" will do right. He will not "do wickedness," "commit iniquity" or "pervert justice," but instead will render unto each strictly according to his work (10–12). When one reasons over such a case as Job's, this is the place to start—and no view can be correct that would overturn this rock solid foundation.

What, then, is the relationship of verses 13–15 to this principle? At first I thought Elihu must be proving the position taken in verses 10–12, though I certainly had a problem figuring out how verses 13–15 were a proof of verses 10–12. Whatever the relationship, it must be drawn from the implications of the statements, and that puts a heavy burden on the interpreter. No wonder different commentators see it in different ways.

But the fact is, the position taken in verses 10–12 do not require proof for anybody in Elihu's audience, even Job, but particularly not for the "men of understanding" specially being addressed. Remember that Elihu is responding to a specific position attributed to Job (5f). Job seemed to be making a judgment about God's actions in his case. It is in that light that verses 13–15 must be explained.

"Who gave him a charge over the earth?" (13a)—*i.e.*, who is his overlord to whom he is responsible, and who judges of his performance in carrying out his assigned task? The very question exposes the absurdity of a mere man being in position to sit in judgment on God's performance—especially when one considers the relation between God and men. All humanity is entirely dependent upon him, not only for its original creation, but also for the continuation of life. Were he to recall the breath of life which he has given (*cf.* Gen 2.7), all flesh would die together (14f).

Is it one of *these*, then, that presumes to sit in judgment upon God as an overlord who assigns to God his task and who, by virtue of his position, rates God's performance? Let us all have a good laugh.

Continuation of the Argument Specially Addressed to Job: The Justice of God in Its Actual Operation (34.16–20)

¹⁶If now *thou hast* understanding [Or, Only understand], hear this:
Hearken to the voice of my words.
¹⁷Shall even one that hateth justice govern?
And wilt thou condemn him that is righteous *and* mighty?-
¹⁸*Him* that saith to a king, *Thou art* vile,
Or to nobles, *Ye are* wicked; [The Heb. as pointed reads, *Is it fit to say to a king, Thou art vile? Or, to nobles, Ye are wicked.*]
¹⁹That respecteth not the persons of princes,
Nor regardeth the rich more than the poor;
For they all are the work of his hands.
²⁰In a moment they die, even at midnight; [Or, and at midnight the people *etc.*]
The people are shaken and pass away,
And the mighty are taken away without hand.

Now Elihu does not address "men of understanding" generally (as in 10) but Job specifically (as indicated by the singular "thou" in 17b). The questions of verse 17 indicate where Elihu's argument is heading. Observe particularly the question whether Job will condemn God (17b), which is repeated in a more general way at a later stage in the question whether anyone can condemn God (29a). This question is at the heart of Elihu's answer to Job in chapter 34.

Consider the two questions of verse 17. First: "Shall even one that hates justice govern?" So Job's assertions (5f) seem to imply. Then further: "And will you condemn him that is righteous *and* mighty?"—this one who shows his *righteousness* by sitting in judgment upon the mighty of earth in a manner that is entirely impartial, not showing favoritism toward rulers or the wealthy, since they as much as the poor are, alike, "the work of his hands" (18f); who shows his *might* by bringing such mighty ones down, as well as the people under their control (20).

These are the ones usually favored by earthly rulers. But if God shows such impartial justice with respect to even these, how can his justice be called into question?

Justice Beyond Reproof Assured by Absolute Knowledge (34.21–30)

²¹For his eyes are upon the ways of a man,
And he seeth all his goings.
²²There is no darkness, nor thick gloom,

Where the workers of iniquity may hide themselves.
²³For he needeth not further to consider a man,
That he should go before God in judgment.
²⁴He breaketh in pieces mighty men *in ways* past finding out [Or, without
    inquisition],
And setteth others in their stead.
²⁵Therefore he taketh knowledge of their works;
And he overturneth them in the night, so that they are destroyed [Heb.
    crushed].
²⁶He striketh them as wicked men
In the open sight of others [Heb. *in the place of beholders*];
²⁷Because they turned aside from following him,
And would not have regard to any of his ways:
²⁸So that they caused the cry of the poor to come unto him,
And he heard the cry of the afflicted [Or, That they might cause… and that
    he might hear].
²⁹When he giveth quietness, who then can condemn?
And when he hideth his face, who then can behold him?
Alike whether *it be done* unto a nation, or unto a man:
³⁰That the godless man reign not,
That there be none to ensnare the people.

Elihu continues to have especially in mind God's judgment upon rulers
and mighty men who misuse their position and cause misery to others
(24–30). It is through such judgments that God's impartial justice is most
clearly made known. Elihu's conclusion is again brought out with questions (29–30).

1. *Omniscience the Basis of God's Impartial Judgments (21–23).* These
verses explain how God is able to judge each man "according to his ways"
(11) and to deal effectively and impartially with all. He knows man's ways,
wherever he goes (21), and no one can hide from him (22). Since he has
such knowledge he needs no prolonged consideration before bringing a
man to justice (23).

2. *Application to the Crushing of Mighty Men (24–25).* Observe—and
this is true all the way through verse 30—that Elihu's eye is upon God's
judgments upon the mighty rulers of earth. These judgments upon the
high and mighty of earth, more than anything, are proof of the impartial
justice of God.

Since God has such knowledge as described (21–23), he destroys
mighty men "without inquisition" (ASV margin) or "investigation" (RSV),

which he finds unnecessary due to his absolute knowledge and changes the established order by putting others in their place (24). So, taking note of their works, God overthrows them in the night (25).

3. *Such Judgments Due to Evil Works (26–28)*. The blow is struck on the basis of God's knowledge of their works, which are evil. They disregarded God's ways and abused their position by oppressing the poor, whose cry came up before God.

4. *Such Divine Judgments Beyond Criticism (29–30)*. With these verses, the answer to Job's position (5f) reaches its culmination and conclusion.

The questions of 29 form a conclusion drawn from the manner of God's dealings described in the previous verses: "When he gives quietness," referring to the peaceful condition that results from the crushing of tyrants and the cessation of their oppression (*cf.* Isa 14.7 in context), "who then can condemn?" (29a). The judgments brought against such powerful oppressors manifest the unmistakeable justice of God.

The providing of "quietness" refers to the benefit that comes from the fall of an oppressive regime. The other question (29b) refers to God's treatment of the tyrant himself: "And when he hides his face," *i.e.* withdraws his favor, acts in a hostile manner toward one (*cf.* 13.24), "who then can behold him?" God's withdrawal of favor is effective. No one can enjoy the favor of God or the blessing of his presence if God has hidden his face from him (*cf.* 2 Sam 14.28, 32; 1 Kgs 10.8; Psa 17.15; 24.3; Matt 18.10; Rev 21.4). Thus God's judgments manifest both righteousness (29a) and might (29b), the two qualities of God that stand out from the beginning of the discussion (17b).

The relation of verses 29c–30 seems a little awkward, but 29c seems to say that what has been said is true no matter whether a nation or a man is involved, and 30 gives the purpose for which God hides his face—to remove from power the godless man, so that "there be none to ensnare the people."

Conclusion with Regard to Job's Complaint Against God (34.31–37)

³¹For hath any said unto God,
I have borne *chastisement*, I will not offend *any more* [Or, though I offend not]:
³²That which I see not teach thou me:
If I have done iniquity, I will do it no more?
³³Shall his recompense be as thou wilt, that thou refusest it?
For thou must choose, and not I:

Therefore speak what thou knowest.
³⁴Men of understanding will say unto me,
Yea, every wise man that heareth me:
³⁵Job speaketh without knowledge,
And his words are without wisdom.
³⁶Would that Job were tried unto the end,
Because of his answering like wicked men.
³⁷For he addeth rebellion unto his sin;
He clappeth his hands among us,
And multiplieth his words against God.

1. *The Charge of Discontent with the Divine Recompense (31–33).* Will Job condemn God? (17b). He has, according to Elihu. Who can condemn God? (29a). According to Elihu, that is the effect of Job's charge against God. The evidence is cited again (31–33).

Verses 31f do not seem to be a model confession which Elihu wishes Job would make, but which he has not. Rather, they refer to actual sayings of Job. Verse 31b is best rendered: "I have borne [*i.e.* affliction] without offending [*i.e.*, though I offend not (ASV margin)]. It is substantially the original citation of Job: "My wound is incurable, *though I am* without transgression" (6b). Verse 32 is also the essence of words Job used (*cf.* 6.24; 13.23).

Having provided this reminder of Job's position, Elihu asks: "Shall his recompense be as you wish, that you refuse it?" (33a). Throughout his argument, Elihu refers to God's recompense according to a man's work (11 and afterward, up to this point). He argues that God manifests a justice that no one can take exception to (17b, 29a). Yet that is exactly what Job's cited words amount to. He expressed discontent with God's recompense. It was not such as Job desired, so he refused it instead of humbly submitting to chastisement. Job seems to have put himself in God's place as the one who is qualified to rule and to determine what recompense is suitable. Elihu himself is satisfied with God's rule and shrinks from such audacity (33b). So let Job tell what he knows, and say what God ought to do (33c).

2. *The Verdict of Wise Men on Job's Blasphemous Words (34–37).* Elihu begins by calling upon wise men to join him in rendering a verdict on Job's words (2–4). Having offered his own refutation of Job's position, he expresses confidence that wise men would agree with him in condemning Job's words. He quotes the verdict he imagines men of understanding ren-

dering upon Job's words (34–37). They will judge that Job speaks "without knowledge," "without wisdom" (35). They will wish that he may be tried without limit because of his irreverent talk (36f), the trial, perhaps, being that to which Job was being put by Elihu and wise men (*cf.* 3) rather than a reference to trial by affliction. Their reason is given in verse 37. They will consider his words to be evidence of his guilt, to which he now adds rebellion (37a), which is manifested by clapping his hands among men (37b) and multiplying words against God (37c).

Third Answer to Job: The Profit of Righteousness (35)

Job's Complaint: The Position to be Answered (35.1–4)

Moreover Elihu answered and said,
²Thinkest thou this to be *thy* right,
Or sayest thou, My righteousness is more than God's,
³That thou sayest, What advantage will it be unto thee?
And, What profit shall I have, more than if I had sinned?
⁴I will answer thee,
And thy companions with thee.

Elihu returns to the complaint mentioned in 34.9, that there is no profit in serving God, without a specific reply being given at the time. Now he provides an answer. *Your companions* (or friends) is explained by 34.7–9. Elihu asks Job whether he considers it his legal right to ask such questions. And further: Is he claiming to be more righteous than God?

Elihu's Answer: The Profit of Righteousness (35.5–8)

⁵Look unto the heavens, and see;
And behold the skies, which are higher than thou.
⁶If thou hast sinned, what effectest thou against him?
And if thy transgressions be multiplied, what doest thou unto him?
⁷If thou be righteous, what givest thou him?
Or what receiveth he of thy hand?
⁸Thy wickedness *may hurt* a man as thou art;
And thy righteousness *may profit* a son of man.

What is the profit of righteousness? It is certainly not to God, who is too highly exalted to be affected one way or the other (5). Our sins can do him no damage (6). Our righteousness is no benefit to him (7). So the benefit of righteousness can only be to the man himself: "Your wickedness affects a man such as you, and your righteousness a son of man" (8 in NKJV). So the righteous life is an advantage in itself, regardless of reward (contrast 1.9–11; 2.4f), and the advantage is to the person who lives right.

Elihu's argument assumes that no one is going to challenge the basic premise that the righteous life is better. Job himself expressed his determination to hold on to it (17.9). But the position being challenged is: What advantage is it *to me*? (3). Elihu replies: To whom if not to you?

Unanswered Cries (35.9–13)

⁹By reason of the multitude of oppressions they cry out;
They cry for help by reason of the arm of the mighty.
¹⁰But none saith, Where is God my Maker,
Who giveth songs in the night,
¹¹Who teacheth us more than the beasts of the earth,
And maketh us wiser than the birds of the heavens?
¹²There they cry, but none giveth answer,
Because of the pride of evil men.
¹³Surely God will not hear an empty *cry*,
Neither will the Almighty regard it.

The remainder of the passage addresses the question why Job's outcries to God are not answered. Elihu begins in a general way with reference to the cries of the suffering. If righteousness is an advantage to the righteous person, what about those mentioned by Job (24.12 in context of 24.1–12), who cry out under the heavy hand of an oppressor (9)? Elihu answers that their cry does not represent a genuine seeking of God their Maker (10), who teaches us more than the beasts and makes us wiser than the birds (11). They cry without receiving an answer, "because of the pride of evil men" (12). The last clause explains the reason for the cry, evil men having reference to the oppressors mentioned in verse 12. God will not hear or regard the empty cry of one who does not seek the Maker who has elevated him above the beasts and birds (13), whose cry is therefore nothing more than the empty cry of an animal in pain, the yelp of a hit dog, for example.

Application to Job (35.14–16)

¹⁴How much less when thou sayest thou beholdest him not,
The cause is before him, and thou waitest for him! [Or, thou beholdest him
not? The cause is before him; therefore wait thou for him.]

¹⁵But now, because he hath not visited in his anger,
Neither doth he greatly regard arrogance [Or, *Thou sayest*, He doth not
    greatly regard arrogance. Thus doth *etc.*];
¹⁶Therefore doth Job open his mouth in vanity;
He multiplieth words without knowledge.

Far less can Job expect the Almighty to respond to such vanity (or emptiness) as he has been spewing out.

Fourth Answer to Job: More Words on God's Behalf (36–37)

Throughout, Elihu is concerned to correct false views of God, which he sees either directly stated or implied in the speeches of Job. He continues on to the end in the same vein.

"…He keeps still before him the same great object, namely to present just thoughts of God; but having in the former speeches corrected the false ideas of Job he proceeds now, more positively, to present his own elevated conceptions of the Creator.

"The object of the passage is to extol the greatness of God in all His operations, both among men and in the world" (A. B. Davidson).

Elihu's object at this point is clearly set forth in an introductory passage.

Introduction: Object Set Forth (36.1–4)

Elihu also proceeded, and said,
²Suffer [Heb. *wait for*] me a little, and I will show thee;
For I have yet somewhat to say on God's behalf [Heb. *there are yet words for God*].
³I will fetch my knowledge from afar,
And will ascribe righteousness to my Maker.
⁴For truly my words are not false:
One that is perfect in knowledge is with thee.

There is no mistaking what Elihu proposes to do in the closing portion of his speech. Still more words remain to be spoken for God (2b). As Delitzsch puts it: "What may be said in vindication of God against Job's complaints and accusations is not yet exhausted." In these words yet to be said Elihu, intends to ascribe righteousness to his Maker (3b). The object of these two chapters is, therefore, clearly defined.

Elihu also commends himself as one well qualified to speak on the subject. Job doubted that the friends consulted travelers with wide knowledge of divine providence (21.29). But Elihu claims to have gathered information about the works of God "from afar" (3a). His views are not based upon some localized and perhaps exceptional case. Job should hear him out, for his words "are not false" and he is "perfect in knowledge" (4)—*i.e.,* his knowledge of the subject is complete.

This is a good place to insert a comment with regard to the view I think one must take of Elihu. His claims seem outrageous to many, who feel free to point out defects in Elihu's arguments. But the author (or final editor, if you wish) evidently finds no such faults with Elihu. He provides no answer to Elihu.

This omission is remarkable. Everywhere else the Book of Job is self-correcting. Job answers the friends. Elihu expresses an opinion about the failure of the friends to deal with Job's complaints, and then he himself answers Job. Jehovah responds to Job, putting Job in his place. But no one answers Elihu. If Elihu's views are false or defective, then this is the only place in the book where false views are set forth without an answer being provided. Elihu's claim to be "perfect in knowledge" is allowed to pass without remark.

Let the force of this fact sink in. Is it not presumptuous on the part of latterday commentators to think the author of Job has left a vacuum which they have to fill in order to make the book complete? That is exactly what they are doing when they criticize Elihu. They are writing a new section for Job, comparable to the Elihu section itself—an evaluation of Elihu comparable to Elihu's criticism of the speeches of Job.

Before we reopen the canon and start printing the Bible with this new, longer version of Job, perhaps we should try harder to make sure we understand Elihu and his distinctive role in the book. In my opinion, not only do the scriptures have a completeness as a whole, but each part is complete in itself—*i.e.,* each part is satisfactory for the purpose it is intended to fill. That view implies that Job is complete in itself. It says what it is intended to say. It does not need our additions.

Further Exposition of the Design of Affliction with Special Application to Job (36.5–23)

Purpose of Affliction (36.5–16)

⁵Behold, God is mighty, and despiseth not any:
He is mighty in strength of understanding [Heb. *heart*].

⁶He preserveth not the life of the wicked,
But giveth to the afflicted *their* right.
⁷He withdraweth not his eyes from the righteous:
But with kings upon the throne
He setteth them for ever, and they are exalted.
⁸And if they be bound in fetters,
And be taken in the cords of afflictions;
⁹Then he showeth them their work,
And their transgressions, that they have behaved themselves proudly.
¹⁰He openeth also their ear to instruction,
And commandeth that they return from iniquity.
¹¹If they hearken and serve *him*,
They shall spend their days in prosperity,
And their years in pleasures [Or, pleasantness].
¹²But if they hearken not, they shall perish by the sword [Or, weapons],
And they shall die without knowledge.
¹³But they that are godless in heart lay up anger:
They cry not for help when he bindeth them.
¹⁴They die [Heb. *Their soul dieth*] in youth,
And their life *perisheth* among [Or, like] the unclean [Or, sodomites. See Deut
    23.17.].
¹⁵He delivereth the afflicted by [Or, in] their affliction,
And openeth their ear in oppression [Or, by adversity].
¹⁶Yea, he would have allured thee out of [Heb. *out of the mouth of*] distress
Into a broad place, where there is no straitness;
And that which is set on thy table would be full of fatness.

God's use of affliction was touched on earlier, but as part of Elihu's answer to the complaint that God is treating Job as an enemy and that he "does not give account of any of his matters" (33.13–30). Now the purpose of affliction is brought forward again, but this time as the primary subject of discussion.

1. *God's Discriminating Treatment of Mankind (5–7)*. Job's reply to Bildad's speech (ch 8) included the complaint that God "destroys the perfect and the wicked" (9.22). Elihu asserts that God is mighty but does not regard any as too lowly for his attention (5). His strength of understanding (5b) is manifested by the punishment of the wicked and doing right by the afflicted (6). The righteous receive his full attention, being exalted as kings (7).

2. *Affliction of the Righteous (8–10)*. Sometimes this differentiation be-

tween the wicked and the righteous may not be apparent. The righteous may suffer affliction (8), but God has a benevolent purpose in such affliction. He uses affliction to show the righteous their sin and pride (9) or perhaps to get their attention and turn them from iniquity (10).

3. *Dealing with Affliction (11–14).* The effect of affliction depends on how one reacts to it. Those who hearken to the lesson being taught through affliction are blessed (11), but if not they perish (12). The godless, who react to affliction by cherishing anger against God rather than seeking his help, will perish with the unclean (13–14).

4. *Deliverance Through Affliction (15–16).* God uses affliction as a means of deliverance (15), and this point brings Elihu to speak directly of Job's case and what God wants to do with Job: "He is wooing you from the jaws of distress to a spacious place free from restriction, to the comfort of your table laden with choice food" (16 in NIV; 16a is literally: "…out of the mouth of distress").

Application to Job: Various Warnings and Admonitions with Regard to the Correct Attitude Toward Affliction (36.17–23)

¹⁷But thou art full of [Or, hast filled up] the judgment of the wicked:
Judgment and justice take hold *on thee.*
¹⁸For let not wrath stir thee up against chastisements;
Neither let the greatness of the ransom turn thee aside [Or, Because there is
    wrath, beware lest thou be led away by thy sufficiency].
¹⁹Will thy cry avail, *that thou be* not in distress,
Or all the forces of *thy* strength?
²⁰Desire not the night,
When peoples are cut off [Heb. *go up*] in their place.
²¹Take heed, regard not iniquity:
For this hast thou chosen rather than affliction.
²²Behold, God doeth loftily in his power:
Who is a teacher like unto him?
²³Who hath enjoined him his way?
Or who can say, Thou hast wrought unrighteousness?

These verses are extremely difficult to translate, as one may quickly see by comparing different translations. But the above heading at least seems to be on the right track.

Verse 17a should perhaps be translated with RSV: "But you are full of the judgment on the wicked"—*i.e.*, the judgment that is due the wicked or that one expects to fall upon them—not having responded to God's effort to woo you out of distress.

Verse 18a seems to be a warning against Job's anger at the treatment he received. The "ransom" in 18b seems to be Job's afflictions. Job is cautioned not to let the great price he is having to pay turn him aside. No other ransom will avail—neither his "cry" nor "all the forces of (his) strength" (19).

Job must not desire the night (20), referring to his repeated longing for death (3.20–22; 6.8f; 10.1, 21f). He must not choose iniquity, referring to his complaints against divine justice, rather than affliction (21).

Instead of expressing discontent with the ways of God (*cf.* 34.33), Job should submit to almighty God, recognizing that he is an incomparable teacher (22; *cf.* 9f) whom no one can give direction to or pass judgment upon (23).

The Greatness of God Manifested in his Marvelous Operations in the Atmosphere (36.24–37.24)

The Mighty Works of God (36.24–37.13)

²⁴Remember that thou magnify his work,
Whereof men have sung.
²⁵All men have looked thereon;
Man beholdeth it afar off.
²⁶Behold, God is great, and we know him not;
The number of his years is unsearchable.
²⁷For he draweth up the drops of water,
Which distil in rain from [Heb. *belonging to*] his vapor [Or, the vapor thereof],
²⁸Which the skies pour down
And drop upon man abundantly.
²⁹Yea, can any understand the spreadings of the clouds,
The thunderings of his pavilion?
³⁰Behold, he spreadeth his light around him [Or, thereon];
And he covereth the bottom of the sea [Or, covereth it with the depths of the sea].
³¹For by these he judgeth the peoples;
He giveth food in abundance.
³²He covereth his hands with the lightning [Heb. *light*],
And giveth it a charge [Or, against the assailant] that it strike the mark.
³³The noise thereof telleth concerning him [Or, it],
The cattle also concerning *the storm* that cometh up [Or, him].
¹Yea, at this my heart trembleth,

And is moved out of its place.
²Hear, oh, hear the noise of his voice,
And the sound [Or, muttering] that goeth out of his mouth.
³He sendeth it forth under the whole heaven,
And his lightening [Heb. *light*] unto the ends [Heb. *skirts*] of the earth.
⁴After it a voice roareth;
He thundereth with the voice of his majesty;
And he restraineth not *the lightnings* [Heb. *them*] when his voice is heard.
⁵God thundereth marvellously with his voice;
Great things doeth he, which we cannot comprehend.
⁶For he saith to the snow, Fall thou on the earth;
Likewise to the shower of rain,
And to the showers of his mighty rain.
⁷He sealeth up the hand of every man,
That all men whom he hath made may know *it*.
⁸Then the beasts go into coverts,
And remain in their dens.
⁹Out of the chamber *of the south* cometh the storm,
And cold out of the north [Heb. *scattering* winds].
¹⁰By the breath of God ice is given;
And the breadth of the waters is straitened [Or, congealed].
¹¹Yea, he ladeth the thick cloud with moisture;
He spreadeth abroad the cloud of his lightning:
¹²And it is turned round about by his guidance,
That they may do whatsoever he commandeth them
Upon the face of the habitable world,
¹³Whether it be for correction, or for his land [Or, earth],
Or for lovingkindness, that he cause it to come.

1. *Exhortation to Praise God's Work (36.24–26)*. Elihu closes with illustrations of the marvellous manifestations of divine power in nature. Verses 24–26 open the section with an exhortation which shows the object of this presentation. Elihu calls upon Job to remember to magnify the work of God, which has caused mankind to sing his praises (24). It is a work manifest to all men (25). It manifests a greatness beyond human knowledge (26). This last idea is repeated twice over (29 and 37.5b) and therefore seems to be a key point which Elihu thinks should impress the mind of Job and bring him to the place he needs to be in relation to God.

2. *Illustrations of God's Work (36.27–37.13)*:
(1) "The wonder of the rain drops" (36.27–28, Davidson).
(2) "The marvel of the thunderstorm" (36.29–37.5, Davidson). Con-

sider a few details: the twofold purpose indicated in 36.31; then the effect of the storm on Elihu (37.1), which he, no doubt, expected Job to feel likewise, if he would pay attention (2); finally, on 37.5, recall Job's remark in 26.14.

(3) Snow, rainfall, frost and ice (37.6–10). Observe the effect of such weather conditions on man: "He sealeth up the hand of every man," so that no work can be done, and man is left to reflect on the great things done by God (7; *cf.* 5b).

(4) Movements of the Clouds (37.11–13). Take note of the divine control and the multiple divine purposes.

Some Questions for Job (37.14–20)

¹⁴Hearken unto this, O Job:
Stand still, and consider the wondrous works of God.
¹⁵Dost thou know how God layeth *his charge* upon them,
And causeth the lightning [Heb. *light*] of his cloud to shine?
¹⁶Dost thou know the balancings of the clouds,
The wondrous works of him who is perfect in knowledge?
¹⁷How thy garments are warm [Or, Thou whose garments are *etc.*],
When the earth is still by reason of the south *wind* [Or, When he quieteth
     the earth by the south wind]?
¹⁸Canst thou with him spread out the sky,
Which is strong as a molten mirror?
¹⁹Teach us what we shall say unto him;
For we cannot set *our speech* in order by reason of darkness.
²⁰Shall it be told him that I would speak?
Or should a man wish that he were swallowed up? [Or, If a man speak, surely
     he shall be swallowed up.]

The practical intent of this presentation is brought home to Job in the concluding portion. Job is exhorted to pay attention "and consider the wondrous works of God," letting them duly impress him (14). The questions of verses 15–18 are calculated to impress Job with the transcendence of the God who does such works. Verse 17 should be read as in the RSV: "you whose garments are hot when the earth is still because of the south wind," with the sense: You being such "a helpless victim of forces that God controls" (ICC), do you know about the things indicated in verses 15–16? Can you do as verse 18 indicates?

In view of the surpassing greatness indicated by such wonders, verse

19 demands that Job tell what words are appropriate to address such a one. Is it appropriate to speak as Job has? One might as well wish his own destruction as to wish to come into God's presence and contend with him (20).

Contrast: *The Appropriate Attitude Toward God (37.21–24)*

²¹And now men see not the light which is bright in the skies [Or, cannot look on the light when it is bright in the skies, when the wind hath passed, and cleared them];
But the wind passeth, and cleareth them.
²²Out of the north cometh golden splendor [Heb. *gold*]:
God hath upon him terrible majesty.
²³*Touching* the Almighty, we cannot find him out
He is excellent in power;
And in justice and plenteous righteousness he will not afflict [Or, to justice… he doeth no violence].
²⁴Men do therefore fear him:
He regardeth not any that are wise of heart.

These verses are more understandable if Elihu's illustrations are drawn from the presence of an actual storm. The bright light of the sun is concealed from view by storm clouds until the skies are cleared by the wind (21). Then the sun appears: "Out of the north comes golden splendor," which resembles the brilliance surrounding God himself (22; *cf.* 36.30). Fully comprehending the Almighty is beyond the mind of man. Yet we can be certain of his power and righteousness (23).

A practical inference closes the speech. God being as he is, "men do fear him. He does not regard any that are wise of heart" (24). Let Job take this message to heart (*cf.* 20).

Against those who try to pick Elihu apart—and in effect, to rewrite the book—though the author (or final editor, if you wish) does not, I contend that Elihu does a marvelous job of preparing the heart of Job for the revelation of the Almighty—this from an equal, who does not therefore merely out-talk Job or overwhelm him with divine majesty. Elihu also provides a wonderful introduction for Jehovah, to whose speeches we now turn.

Jehovah's Speeches: Second Stage of Resolution (Job 38.1–42.6)

Job's suffering brought the genuineness of his piety under a searchlight, and put it to a severe test (*cf.* 1.9–11; 2.4–5). By the end of the debate he successfully endured this trial and proved Satan a liar and slanderer. Far from renouncing God, he had clung to God to the end, his faith even increasing (*cf.* 13.7–11; 14.13–15; 16.18–21; 17.3; 19.23–29).

Yet the test was not passed without sin. Specifically, Job accused God of injustice toward himself and in his rule of the world. The speeches of Elihu brought a strong indictment against Job in this regard.

Two objects will be accomplished at the end of the debate. First, Job's complaints needed to be answered, and God's treatment of him to be vindicated. Job's misunderstandings needed to be taken away, and his mind satisfied with regard to his relation to God and God's treatment of him. But God is not going to bring himself before the bar of human justice. He is not going to explain himself or to answer Job's questions. It would not be appropriate for the Judge of all the earth to do so. That was the role of Elihu, and by the end of Elihu's speeches Job's mind is prepared for the manifestation of Jehovah that follows.

Second, Job needs to be humbled, cured of the presumption that led him to question God and God's rule of the world; he needs to be brought to his proper place before God. That is the object of Jehovah's speeches. Jehovah does not manifest himself for the purpose of answering Job's questions or otherwise to explain himself, but to humble Job and bring him to realize his proper place. But neither does he come to destroy Job under the weight of his authority. He comes rather to heal Job's troubled mind and to bring him to repentance. Jehovah accomplishes this second object by a revelation of his own greatness.

Job repeatedly expressed the longing for a chance to contend with God (9:34f; 13.3, 13–28 [esp. 20–24]; 23.3–5; 31.35–37). His last speech reached its climax with a demand that the Almighty respond to his protestation of innocence (31.35–37). Now Jehovah does respond, but not as Job wished. He does not explain himself, but rebukes the presumption that makes such a demand.

Jehovah's First Speech: Indictment of Job for Obscuring Divine Counsel by Ignorant Speech (38.1–40.5)

Opening Challenge (38.1–3)

Then Jehovah answered Job out of the whirlwind, and said,
²Who is this that darkeneth counsel
By words without knowledge?
³Gird up now thy loins like a man;
For I will demand of thee, and declare thou unto me.

It is not unusual for Jehovah to manifest himself in a storm or other natural phenomena (*cf.* Josh 10.11; Psa 18, 29; Hab 3). So it is here. Jehovah answers Job "out of the whirlwind" (1). His opening words, along with the closing demand (40.2), define the purpose of the examination that follows.

Job is accused of darkening counsel, "by words without knowledge" (2). *Counsel* refers to a purpose, design or plan, here "the divine purpose underlying the constitution and maintenance of the world" (ICC), somewhat as the word "wisdom" is applied in 28.23–27; it is about the equivalent of divine providence (AB). Job is accused of obscuring [hiding (in 42.3)] the divine plan by means of ignorant talk. Observe how much attention is given in the speech to Job's deficiency in knowledge. He has overstepped his bounds and spoken out on subjects where his ignorance should have kept him silent.

God has not come to answer Job's questions but to ask him some questions. God's purpose is not to explain himself to Job but to expose the gaps in Job's knowledge, to show that he may not know as much as he thinks he does, and to show him how far out of line he is when he presumptuously questions the rule of the Almighty. Job is challenged to prepare for an examination (3). He wanted to contend with God. Now he has the chance to show how much he knows about the world.

Examination with Regard to the Inanimate Creation: Wonders of Earth and Sky (38.4–38)

Creation of the World (38.4–7)

⁴Where wast thou when I laid the foundations of the earth?
Declare, if thou hast understanding [Heb. *if thou knowest understanding*].
⁵Who determined the measures thereof, if thou knowest [Or, *seeing*]?
Or who stretched the line upon it?

⁶Whereupon were the foundations [Heb. *sockets*] thereof fastened [Heb.
   made to sink]?
Or who laid the corner-stone thereof,
⁷When the morning stars sang together,
And all the sons of God shouted for joy?

God challenges Job to show his understanding (4b) and knowledge (5a).
Creation is compared to the erection of a building. "Where were you when
I laid the foundations of the earth?" (4a). If you were present when I created the world and therefore know so much, tell me about the creation.
Who (in 5–7) does not ask for the identity of the person (see 4a), but calls
upon Job to reflect upon the sort of Being who could have done such
things. The purpose throughout is to make Job see just how much difference there is between himself and God. For the rejoicing at the laying of
the foundations (6f) compare Ezra 3.11b.

Origin of the Sea (38.8–11)

⁸Or *who* shut up the sea with doors,
When it brake forth, *as if* it had issued [Or, and issued] out of the womb;
⁹When I made clouds the garment thereof,
And thick darkness a swaddling-band for it,
¹⁰And marked out [Heb. *brake*] for it my bound,
And set bars and doors,
¹¹And said, Hitherto shalt thou come, but no further;
And here shall thy proud waves be stayed?

The origin of the sea is compared to the birth of a monster needing to be
controlled. Let Job consider the majesty of the One who could, as it were,
lock up the sea with doors and set its bounds.

Commanding Break of Day (38.12–15)

¹²Hast thou commanded the morning since thy days *began*,
And caused the dayspring to know its place;
¹³That it might take hold of the ends of the earth,
And the wicked be shaken out of it?
¹⁴It is changed as clay under the seal;
And *all things* stand forth as a garment [Or, as in a garment]:
¹⁵And from the wicked their light is withholden,
And the high arm is broken.

Have you ever once, since the beginning of your days, commanded the morning and caused the dawn to emerge and fill its place? (12). God does daily what Job has never once done.

The dawning of the day (set forth in 13) takes hold of the ends (literally *skirts*) of the earth and shake the wicked out of it. Consult 24.13–17 for night as the period when the wicked are active (15). Their "light" (15) is darkness (24.17).

The darkness of night deprives the earth of form and color, but with the dawning of day the earth is changed as the impression of the seal (or signet ring) on clay, so that everything stands forth in its proper garb (14).

Depths and Breadth of the Earth (38.16–18)

¹⁶Hast thou entered into the springs of the sea?
Or hast thou walked in the recesses [Or, search] of the deep?
¹⁷Have the gates of death been revealed unto thee?
Or hast thou seen the gates of the shadow of death?
¹⁸Hast thou comprehended the earth in its breadth?
Declare, if thou knowest it all.

Nor has Job explored the depths and sources of the sea (16). Nor does he know much about the gates of death (17). Nor has he comprehended the breadth of the earth (18a). Again, observe the challenge to Job's knowledge: "Declare, if you know it all" (18b).

Once Job responded to the friends' position about the calamitous end to which the wicked come: Have you not asked the travellers, who have seen much more than you? "And do you not know their evidences…?" (21.29). It begins to appear that Job may have missed a few things himself.

Dwelling of Light and Darkness (38.19–21)

¹⁹Where is the way to the dwelling of light?
And as for darkness, where is the place thereof,
²⁰That thou shouldest take it to the bound thereof,
And that thou shouldest discern the paths to the house thereof?
²¹*Doubtless*, thou knowest, for thou wast then born,
And the number of thy days is great!

God separated light from darkness at the beginning (Gen 1.3–5). But where does the light go when it is dark? And where the darkness when it is light? Can Job escort these home? (19f). All such questions are, of course, a poetic way of asking about the ultimate causes of things.

These questions are but another challenge to Job's knowledge (21), impressing upon him the need "to accept his limitations and to let God be God" (Anderson).

Snow, Hail, Light and Wind (38.22–24)

²²Hast thou entered the treasuries of the snow,
Or hast thou seen the treasures of the hail,
²³Which I have reserved against the time of trouble,
Against the day of battle and war?
²⁴By what way is the light parted [Or, Which is the way *to the place* where the
   light is *etc.*],
Or the east wind scattered upon the earth?

A few other things Job's research has missed! Has he been to the place where God keeps the snow and the hail stored up, so that they might be used at the time he chooses to use them in battle and war against the enemy? (22f). No, Job has not explored this arsenal.

In this context, Anderson thinks we should recall the use of light for lightning in Elihu's last speech (36.30, 32; 37.3, 11), so that verse 24 would refer to two more elements of the divine arsenal. In any case, the main point is that these are two more things of which Job is ignorant.

Rain, Dew, Ice and Frost (38.25–30)

²⁵Who hath cleft a channel for the waterflood,
Or the way for the lightning of the thunder;
²⁶To cause it to rain on a land where no man is;
On the wilderness, wherein there is no man;
²⁷To satisfy the waste and desolate *ground*,
And to cause the tender grass [Or, greensward] to spring forth?
²⁸Hath the rain a father?
Or who hath begotten the drops of dew?
²⁹Out of whose womb came the ice?
And the hoary frost of heaven, who hath gendered it [Or, given it birth]?
³⁰The waters hide themselves *and become* like stone [Or, are congealed
   like stone],
And the face of the deep is frozen [Heb. *cohereth*].

Who has directed the flow of the water and the lightning that attends it, so that rain falls on wilderness land where no man lives and grass springs forth? (25–27). Man would not be likely to think of such a thing, even if he were capable of doing it. Once his own needs are supplied, he has no thought of providing water for a place where no human beings even lived. The range of things to which God gives attention seems to go way beyond what concerns Job or men generally.

Nor does the rain, the dew, ice or the frost have a human source (28–29). Verse 30 describes the formation of ice from the waters.

Stars in Their Constellations (38.31–33)

³¹Canst thou bind the cluster [Or, chain; Or, sweet influences] of the Pleiades,
Or loose the bands of Orion?
³²Canst thou lead forth the Mazzaroth [Or, the signs of the Zodiac] in their
season?
Or canst thou guide the Bear with her train [Heb. *sons*]?
³³Knowest thou the ordinances of the heavens?
Canst thou establish the dominion thereof in the earth?

Reference to constellations is obvious, as all scholarly commentators seem to agree. Other than that, however, these verses contain many uncertainties. Even the identity of the constellations is debatable. The point, however, is clear: Job is asked whether these are under his control. Again the vast distance between God and a man like Job is impressed. Consult Genesis 1.16–18 on verse 33.

Rain for a Thirsty Earth (38.34–38)

³⁴Canst thou lift up thy voice to the clouds,
That abundance of waters may cover thee?
³⁵Canst thou send forth lightnings, that they may go,
And say unto thee, Here we are?
³⁶Who hath put wisdom in the inward parts [Or, dark clouds]?
Or who hath given understanding to the mind [Or, meteor]?
³⁷Who can number the clouds by wisdom?
Or who can pour out [Heb. *cause to lie down*] the bottles of heaven,
³⁸When the dust runneth into a mass,
And the clods cleave fast together?

Can you command the clouds to give forth abundance of waters? (34).

What about the lightnings? Will they present themselves to you as obedient servants? (35).

Verse 36 is uncertain. It is difficult to explain, in the context, whether the reference is to human wisdom and understanding or to animal instincts. The latter would seem to be natural, if only these questions followed verse 38.

Who can number the clouds? (37a) They may seem ever so many, but who can cause these skin bottles to tilt so that water is poured out (37b) when the earth so desperately needs it (38; *cf.* Lev 26.19; Deut 28.23).

Marvels in the World of Animal Life (38.39–39.30)

Prey for Lion and Raven (38.39–41)

³⁹**Canst thou hunt the prey for the lioness,**
Or satisfy the appetite of the young lions,
⁴⁰**When they couch in their dens,**
And **abide in the covert to lie in wait?**
⁴¹**Who provideth for the raven his prey,**
When his young ones cry unto God,
And **wander for lack of food?**

Are you responsible for the instinct by which these creatures are able to find prey for their young? What God has done for all his creatures certainly goes beyond anything possible to man.

The Mountain Goat (39.1–4)

Knowest thou the time when the wild goats of the rock bring forth?
Or **canst thou mark when the hinds do calve?**
²**Canst thou number the months that they fulfil?**
Or knowest thou the time when they bring forth?
³**They bow themselves, they bring forth their young,**
They cast out their pains.
⁴**Their young ones become strong, they grow up in the open field;**
They go forth, and return not again [Or, return not unto them].

Job had been a wealthy man with great herds of sheep, camels, oxen and donkeys (1.3) and doubtless knew a lot about the breeding of such domesticated animals. But what does he know about the wild goats which are so inaccessible to mankind? Again we recall Job's question to the friends (in

21.29): Have you consulted the travellers? The friends are not alone when it comes to having limited experience and knowledge.

The Wild Donkey (39.5–8)

⁵Who hath sent out the wild ass free?
Or who hath loosed the bonds of the swift ass,
⁶Whose home I have made the wilderness,
And the salt land his dwelling--place?
⁷He scorneth the tumult of the city,
Neither heareth he the shoutings of the driver [Or, taskmaster].
⁸The range of the mountains is his pasture,
And he searcheth after every green thing.

Who made such a creature only to let him run wild and free, not subject to master nor dependent on one? God's purposes certainly seem to go beyond the uses of mankind.

The Wild Ox (39.9–12)

⁹Will the wild-ox be content to serve thee?
Or will he abide by thy crib?
¹⁰Canst thou bind the wild-ox with his band in the furrow?
Or will he harrow the valleys after thee?
¹¹Wilt thou trust him, because his strength is great?
Or wilt thou leave to him thy labor?
¹²Wilt thou confide in him, that he will bring home thy seed,
And gather *the grain* of thy threshing-floor?

His strength is certainly useful in man's service. But mankind has not been able to bring him into subjection and cannot trust him to do as he wishes.

The Ostrich (39.13–18)

¹³The wings of the ostrich wave proudly;
But are they the pinions and plumage of love [Or, a stork]?
¹⁴For she leaveth her eggs on the earth,
And warmeth them in the dust,
¹⁵And forgetteth that the foot may crush them,
Or that the wild beast may trample them.

¹⁶She dealeth hardly with [Or, is hardened against] her young ones, as if they
  were not hers:
Though her labor be in vain, *she is* without fear;
¹⁷Because God hath deprived her of wisdom [Heb. *made her to forget wisdom*],
Neither hath he imparted to her understanding.
¹⁸What time she lifteth up herself on high [Or, rouseth herself up to flight],
She scorneth the horse and his rider.

What a strange creature! Can Job explain it? Might God's creation not include a great deal that is incomprehensible to mankind?

The War Horse (39.19–25)

¹⁹Hast thou given the horse *his* might?
Hast thou clothed his neck with the quivering mane [Heb. *shaking*]?
²⁰Hast thou made him to leap as a locust?
The glory of his snorting is terrible.
²¹He paweth [Heb. *They paw*] in the valley, and rejoiceth in his strength:
He goeth out to meet the armed men [Or, the weapons].
²²He mocketh at fear, and is not dismayed;
Neither turneth he back from the sword.
²³The quiver rattleth against [Or, upon] him,
The flashing spear and the javelin.
²⁴He swalloweth the ground with fierceness and rage;
Neither believeth he that it is the voice of the trumpet [Or, standeth still
  at *etc.*].
²⁵As oft as the trumpet *soundeth* he saith, Aha!
And he smelleth the battle afar off,
The thunder of the captains, and the shouting.

Take note of the question. Is it Job that created such a magnificent animal? The creator of the horse seems to be much more than a man.

The Hawk and the Eagle (39.26–30)

²⁶Is it by thy wisdom that the hawk soareth,
(And) stretcheth her wings toward the south?
²⁷Is it at thy command that the eagle mounteth up,
And maketh her nest on high?
²⁸On the cliff she dwelleth, and maketh her home,
Upon the point of the cliff, and the stronghold.

²⁹**From thence she spieth out the prey;**
Her eyes behold it afar off.
³⁰**Her young ones also suck up blood:**
And where the slain are, there is she.

Again it is important to pay attention to God's questions about the creation: "Is it by your wisdom...?" (26). "Is it at your command...?" (27). Attention is focused throughout on the great intellectual gulf between God and man.

Application: Repetition of the Challenge to Job (40.1–2)

Moreover Jehovah answered Job, and said,
²**Shall he that cavilleth contend with the Almighty?**
He that argueth with God, let him answer it.

The speech closes as it opened, with a challenge to Job. "Shall the fault-finder contend with the Almighty?" (RSV; NASB). The question, together with the demand for an answer (2), reinforces the purpose of the examination. It brings the speech to bear on Job who finds fault with divine providence. Does he, after this exhibition of the divine glory and the manifoldness of the divine wisdom, still wish to contend with God? (*cf.* 9.3; 13.3). Does he still think he knows enough to sit in judgment on divine providence?

Job is called the one who argues with (ASV, RSV, NEB), reproves (KJV, NASB), rebukes (NKJV) or corrects God. Jehovah demands that he answer his questions.

Job's Response: The Effect Produced by this Revelation of God (40.3–5)

³**Then Job answered Jehovah, and said,**
⁴**Behold, I am of small account; What shall I answer thee?**
I lay my hand upon my mouth.
⁵**Once have I spoken, and I will not answer;**
Yea, twice, but I will proceed no further.

The examination had the effect of humbling Job before God. He confesses himself to be "light," "insignificant" (NASB), "of small account" (ASV, RSV), having no answer to offer. He lays his hand upon his mouth and confesses, in effect, that he has said too much already.

So Job has to confess that he does not know as much as he thought he did. In fact, no man knows enough to "contend with the Almighty."

Jehovah's Second Reply to Job (40.6–42.6)

Job's response (40.3–5) is an acknowledgment that he has been in over his head; that he has been spouting forth ignorance (*cf.* 39.2); that he had best shut his mouth, for he has already said too much. But his confession must go further. He not only spoke ignorantly. He spoke sinfully as well. He presumed to criticize Jehovah's rule, implying that he knew better. That, I think, is the reason for Jehovah's second speech. Job must be convicted of his outrageous presumption in daring to criticize Jehovah's rule of the world.

Not only does Job not know enough to understand the world nor have the power to do the things in which God's hand is so evident, but he has not the least capability of getting justice done, even if he were appointed ruler of the world. God exposes Job's disability by inviting him to try his hand at ruling the world, setting things right and establishing justice in the world. The invitation is followed by an exposure of how little Job is capable of accepting the invitation. Thus the second speech convicts Job of what his criticism of God actually amounts to, impresses his heart with just how far he has overstepped his bounds, and produces a confession not only of ignorance but of serious sin to go with it.

The first reply addressed generally the outrageous gall of proposing to contend with God (*cf.* esp. 40.1–2). The second is more specific, dealing with the preposterous attempt to sit in judgment on God and the righteousness of God's government (40.6–9) as a particular aspect of contending with God (41.10–11). This aspect of Jehovah's answer to Job is introduced with another opening statement (40.6–14).

Opening Challenge and Definition of Issues (40.6–14)

Job's Presumption Challenged (40.6–9)

⁶Then Jehovah answered Job out of the whirlwind, and said,
⁷Gird up thy loins now like a man:
I will demand of thee, and declare thou unto me.
⁸Wilt thou even annul my judgment?
Wilt thou condemn me, that thou mayest be justified?
⁹Or hast thou an arm like God?
And canst thou thunder with a voice like him?

God introduces the second challenge to Job with the same words as the first (7 with 38.3). But after that the new, more specific issue is broached. Job's speeches presumed to challenge the way God runs the world. He presumed, in effect, to cancel out the divine judgment. So Jehovah challenges him on that point (8a). Job argued his own innocence, vindicating himself at the cost of putting God in the wrong and condemning God. So that point is the basis of another challenge (8b).

But if one is going to take over the role of judge he must not only have moral integrity, but also the power to implement his judgments. So Job is challenged to say whether he has power like that of God (9).

Proposal of an Experiment Putting Job's Presumption to the Test (40.10–14)

¹⁰Deck thyself now with excellency and dignity;
And array thyself with honor and majesty.
¹¹Pour forth the overflowings of thine anger;
And look upon every one that is proud, and abase him.
¹²Look on every one that is proud, *and* bring him low;
And tread down the wicked where they stand.
¹³Hide them in the dust together;
Bind their faces in the hidden *place*.
¹⁴Then will I also confess of thee
That thine own right hand can save thee.

Jehovah ironically invites Job to put on the royal robes; to clothe himself with the attributes of the supreme ruler; to take over the government and undertake the rule of the world, bringing down the wicked and burying them in the dust (10–13). Job's presumptuous proposals implied that he is qualified for the job. "So, go to it," Jehovah challenges. The challenge is tantamount to saying: "All right, Job. Now is your chance. Let us see what you can do."

The challenge is devastating to Job. It reveals the real essence of Job's positions; it shows Job how far he is from being equal to such a task and puts him in his proper place before God.

The opening challenge ends with the confession Jehovah is prepared to make if Job succeeds at the undertaking to which he is challenged (14). The language of 14b recalls verses 8 and 9. The salvation referred to is vindication from all charges, acquittal from guilt (8b, which is linked to 9). This is the salvation Job sought all along. He wants to be cleared of the charges against him—charges directly expressed by the friends and implied, he thought, in God's treatment of him. Compare also 13.16 for the use of the word "salvation" in a similar context.

Behemoth and Leviathan (40.15–41.34)

Can Job do it? Will he be equal to the task which he is challenged to undertake? And, ultimately, the question that is proposed is: Is Job really up to contending with God and thus establishing his innocence and vindicating himself from the unjust treatment at the hands of God, of which he complained?

Before he takes God on, perhaps he better get some experience first by trying his hand at subduing a couple of God's creatures. If he cannot subdue Behemoth and Leviathan, what hope of success will he have when it comes to contending with God?

This connection of thought is most clearly expressed at 41.10–11.

Behemoth (40.15–24)

¹⁵Behold now, behemoth [That is, the hippotamus], which I made as well as [Heb. *with*] thee;
He eateth grass as an ox.
¹⁶Lo now, his strength is in his loins,
And his force is in the muscles of his belly.
¹⁷He moveth his tail like a cedar:
The sinews of his thighs are knit together.
¹⁸His bones are *as* tubes of brass;
His limbs [Or, ribs] are like bars of iron.
¹⁹He is the chief of the ways of God:
He *only* that made him giveth him his sword.
²⁰Surely the mountains bring him forth food,
Where all the beasts of the field do play.
²¹He lieth under the lotus-trees,
In the covert of the reed, and the fen.
²²The lotus-trees cover him with their shade;
The willows of the brook compass him about.
²³Behold, if a river overflow [Or, be violent], he trembleth not;
He is confident, though a Jordan swell even to his mouth.
²⁴Shall any take him when he is on the watch,
Or pierce through his nose with a snare?

The Hebrew is the plural of the word for beast. The reference in every passage except this one is to cattle, animals or beasts. But the description here suggests a specific animal. The plural seems to have intensive force and to mean something like "great beast." Though some think of the elephant, since Bochart most interpreters identify Behemoth with the hippotamus. But others think of the dinosaur. Perhaps we cannot be sure, but does it matter? The main point seems to remain the same, whatever this monstrous animal is.

Most of the passage is descriptive of this creature and his habits. The last verse (24) seems to bring out the point, namely, the difficulty of subduing this monstrous beast, especially when compared with the beginning of the leviathan passage (41.1–11).

Leviathan (Job 41 [40.25 in Hebrew])

Canst thou draw out leviathan [That is, the crocodile] with a fishhook?
Or press down his tongue with a cord?
²Canst thou put a rope [Heb. *a rope of rushes*] into his nose?
Or pierce his jaw through with a hook [Or, spike]?
³Will he make many supplications unto thee?
Or will he speak soft words unto thee?
⁴Will he make a covenant with thee,
That thou shouldest take him for a servant for ever?
⁵Wilt thou play with him as with a bird?
Or wilt thou bind him for thy maidens?
⁶Will the bands *of fishermen* make traffic of him?
Will they part him among the merchants?
⁷Canst thou fill his skin with barbed irons,
Or his head with fish-spears?
⁸Lay thy hand upon him;
Remember the battle, and do so no more.
⁹ [ch 41.1 in Heb.] Behold, the hope of him is in vain:
Will not one be cast down even at the sight of him?
¹⁰None is so fierce that he dare stir him up;
Who then is he that can stand before me?
¹¹Who hath first given unto me, that I should repay him?
Whatsoever is under the whole heaven is mine.
¹²I will not keep silence concerning his limbs,
Nor his mighty strength, nor his goodly frame.
¹³Who can strip off his outer garment [Heb. *uncover the face of his garment*]?
Who shall come within his jaws?
¹⁴Who can open the doors of his face?
Round about his teeth is terror [Or, His teeth are terrible round about].

¹⁵*His* strong scales [Or, courses of scales: Heb. *channels of shields*] are *his* pride,
Shut up together *as with* a close seal.
¹⁶One is so near to another,
That no air can come between them.
¹⁷They are joined one to another;
They stick together, so that they cannot be sundered.
¹⁸His sneezings flash forth light,
And his eyes are like the eyelids of the morning.
¹⁹Out of his mouth go burning torches,
And sparks of fire leap forth.
²⁰Out of his nostrils a smoke goeth,
As of a boiling pot and *burning* rushes.
²¹His breath kindleth coals,
And a flame goeth forth from his mouth.
²²In his neck abideth strength,
And terror danceth before him.
²³The flakes of his flesh are joined together:
They are firm upon him; they cannot be moved.
²⁴His heart is as firm as a stone;
Yea, firm as the nether millstone.
²⁵When he raiseth himself up, the mighty are afraid:
By reason of consternation they are beside themselves.
²⁶If one lay at him with the sword, it cannot avail;
Nor the spear, the dart, nor the pointed shaft [Or, coat of mail].
²⁷He counteth iron as straw,
And brass as rotten wood.
²⁸The arrow [Heb. *son of the bow*] cannot make him flee:
Sling-stones are turned with him into stubble.
²⁹Clubs are counted as stubble:
He laugheth at the rushing of the javelin.
³⁰His underparts are *like* sharp potsherds:
He spreadeth *as it were* a threshing-wain upon the mire.
³¹He maketh the deep to boil like a pot:
He maketh the sea like a pot of ointment.
³²He maketh a path to shine after him;
One would think the deep to be hoary.
³³Upon earth there is not his like,
That is made without fear.
³⁴He beholdeth everything that is high:
He is king over all the sons of pride.

The name Leviathan occurs in five passages of the Old Testament. Here the term occurs "not in reference to some mythical monster of the past but, as attested by the context, of an actual living animal of the present; it is used as a designation of the crocodile, which is there described in poetic language, even as breathing fire and smoke."

Almost all the chapter is descriptive of this ferocious creature. But the key verses, so far as the purpose and main point of the passage are concerned, are 10 and 11.

Thrust of the Argument (10–11)

These verses give the application of the whole passage. The first question (10b) relates to one's ability to contend with God (*cf.* 40.2). Job repeatedly expressed the desire to stand before God and argue his case. He was confident of the outcome as he demanded answers of God. But if a man cannot contend with the crocodile, how can he stand before God?

Job thought sure he would be vindicated if only he had a fair chance to prove his case. It would then be clear that he was being wronged, that God was treating him unfairly. But the other question implies that God owes no one anything. No one has given anything to God that has brought God into debt to him. What could it be, since everything in the world belongs to God? (11).

Consider how this question speaks to Job's complaint. The complaint was that he was not being treated fairly, that his suffering involved a perversion of justice, implied by the fact that he was not receiving his due—something that was his by right; something owed to him. In fact the whole theology held by Job and his friends that connected suffering with sin and prosperity with piety in such an absolute manner would seem to imply that prosperity was the "due" of a pious man. I feel confident that the friends, had they known of Job's innocence, would have concluded as Job did that his case involved a perversion of justice.

Recall that Job's main problem is not the physical suffering, but the psychological problem growing out of his perception that God is treating him as a sinner. He is simply outraged that he, as a man of integrity, should be treated as the worst sort of sinner. There was no justice in it.

Relate now the question of these verses to the opening challenge of this second speech (40.6–14, but esp. 8, 9 and 14). Observe that these verses present the only conclusion drawn from the argumentation connected with the hypopotamus and the crocodile. The message that Jehovah wants to impress upon Job, it begins to appear, is that salvation (in the sense defined by the context, *i.e.*, justification, vindication from all wrong) is a gift of God and not something owed to man.

What has Job done to bring God into debt to him? God owes him nothing. Job's prosperity at the beginning was not something God owed him as a righteous man. When it was taken away, it was not a matter of depriving Job of something that was his by right. Whatever one has is a gift of God's free grace.

Job's Response (42.1–6)

Then Job answered Jehovah, and said,
²I know that thou canst do all things,
And that no purpose of thine can be restrained.
³Who is this that hideth counsel without knowledge?
Therefore have I uttered that which I understood not,
Things too wonderful for me, which I knew not.
⁴Hear, I beseech thee, and I will speak;
I will demand of thee, and declare thou unto me.
⁵I had heard of thee by the hearing of the ear;
But now mine eye seeth thee:
⁶Wherefore I abhor *myself*,
And repent in dust and ashes.

Job's response shows the impressions the revelation of God has made on him:

Acknowledgment of God's Competence to Fulfill His Purposes (2)

The first impression is that God is an intelligent Being who purposes and then acts—One fully capable of carrying his purposes into effect (2). Much in the operations going on in the world seems without rhyme or reason. But not so. God is steadily at work, bringing his purposes to pass.

Confession of His Own Limitations (3)

Verse 3a alludes to Jehovah's question (38.2). Job raises the question again in order to confess that he is in over his head, and had obscured the divine counsel by spouting off his ignorance.

Fuller Understanding of God (4–5)

Verse 4 alludes to 38.3 and 40.7, which, in turn, were the answer to Job's longing (13.22). Job realizes now that he did not know what he was asking. All his spouting off was foolishness based on an extremely limited knowledge of God. Compared to the clear vision of God he now has, his former knowledge is like hearsay information. Verse 5, however, does not imply physical vision, "but an experience of God that was real and personal" (Rowley).

Repudiation of Former Ignorance (6)

Should the thought be completed with "myself" or with "it," referring to Job's former presumptuous speech? Either view comes to about the same thing. But context suggests that his ignorant talk is the object (3).

Epilogue: The Vindication of Job (42.7–17)

God's Wrath Against the Friends (42.7–9)

⁷And it was so, that, after Jehovah had spoken these words unto Job, Jehovah said to Eliphaz the Temanite, My wrath is kindled against thee, and against thy two friends; for ye have not spoken of me the thing that is right, as my servant Job hath. ⁸Now therefore, take unto you seven bullocks and seven rams, and go to my servant Job, and offer up for yourselves a burnt-offering; and my servant Job shall pray for you; for him will I accept, that I deal not with you after your folly; for ye have not spoken of me the thing that is right, as my servant Job hath. ⁹So Eliphaz the Temanite and Bildad the Shuhite and Zophar the Naamathite went, and did according as Jehovah commanded them: and Jehovah accepted Job.

Observe the reason for God's wrath against the three friends: "for you have not spoken of me the thing that is right, as my servant Job has" (7b, 8d). Reference is not to the speeches of the friends or of Job. Much in the speeches of both was rebuked as erroneous—especially Job's, but the friends' also, though only by Elihu. Reference can only be to Job's confession (1–6)—a confession which was not made by the friends, though it should have been, for they were in over their heads as much as Job was. Their speeches were just as much a reflection on God as Job's, even though they intended to honor God. The view they took implied that the sufferings of a pious man would be a miscarriage of justice, just as much as

Job had accused God of injustice. So they have every bit as much reason for repentance as Job. But their confession is not forthcoming as Job's is, though they do finally follow Jehovah's direction (8f).

Job's Restoration (42.10–17)

¹⁰**And Jehovah turned the captivity of Job, when he prayed for his friends: and Jehovah gave Job twice as much as he had before. ¹¹Then came there unto him all his brethren, and all his sisters, and all they that had been of his acquaintance before, and did eat bread with him in his house: and they bemoaned him, and comforted him concerning all the evil that Jehovah had brought upon him: every man also gave him a piece of money [Heb. *kesitah*], and every one a ring of gold. ¹²So Jehovah blessed the latter end of Job more than his beginning: And he had fourteen thousand sheep, and six thousand camels, and a thousand yoke of oxen, and a thousand she-asses. ¹³He had also seven sons and three daughters. ¹⁴And he called the name of the first, Jemimah: and the name of the second, Keziah; and the name of the third, Keren-happuch. ¹⁵And in all the land were no women found so fair as the daughters of Job: and their father gave them inheritance among their brethren. ¹⁶And after this Job lived a hundred and forty years, and saw his sons, and his sons' sons, *even* four generations. ¹⁷So Job died, being old and full of days.**

The latter end is good. Job is rewarded at last. But James 5.11 has identified the point precisely. The restoration of Job is an expression of God's pity and mercy. It is not the payment of a debt.

Thus the trial is over. Job again lives in prosperity. But he undoubtedly looks upon his blessings with new eyes. He sees everything as gifts of God's grace, expressions of undeserved favor, rather than as the payment of a debt owed to him.

The Answer to Satan's Taunts

Satan charged that even the best man on earth would not serve God without reward. The charge was a slur on the genuineness of Job's piety, but also a reflection on God.

It is important to notice that Job acknowledges God even before being restored to prosperity. His expressions give the testimony of the best man on earth to the glory of God. Job's answer to Satan is that God is so great he ought to be revered and served simply because of who he is and without regard to reward.

This understanding is tantamount to an acknowledgment of justification by grace, which is so much involved in Jehovah's examination of Job. Job expresses the understanding that God owed him nothing. His works do not bring God into debt to him. Anything done for him is pure grace, not payment of a debt but entirely gratuitous.

Final Thoughts

No. 1. Some may imagine that the rewards given to Job at the end go against the overall thesis of the book and the final resolution of the problem. Is it not finally a capitulation to the view of the friends? Not to any misapplications of principle they have made, I would say. In fact the friends were mostly right. It is better, even more rewarding, to serve God even in this life, not to speak of the afterlife. That point was never in question. All the speakers agree.

In fact, would most principled people not agree that there is a right (or better) way to live? One that leads to a better, more prosperous and secure life? Who would not say so? All of us choose the way of life we think is best for us.

But whether to make our own prosperity the aim and purpose of life is another matter. Should we not serve God as the priority regardless of reward? Otherwise piety (*i.e.,* respect or devotion to God) is no real piety but merely a serving of self.

Such are the issues put before us in Job.

The problem arose from the obscurity of divine providence and apparent exceptions to the rule.

The rule is set down in the Pentateuch, for example, which assures us that the person who lives a faithful life will have a better life, a more prosperous life, than otherwise. But none of this is arbitrary. It is a matter of cause and effect. Obey your parents and it will keep you out of a lot of trouble, to choose one fairly obvious example. But we are not in heaven yet. We live in a world of cause and effect where a lot of things have gone wrong. It is a world under a curse (Gen 3). Obedient children can still be killed by drunken drivers and so forth. God does not arbitrarily intervene and make the world different than it is in every particular case. And so, exceptions to the rule are found.

But mankind has contradictory desires. We want freedom; we do not want to be controlled. But living in a world of freedom has consequences. When the consequences come, then we want something else. We wonder why God does not control everything and see to it that no suffering comes to us. We cannot have it both ways.

No. 2. Job was never answered. He was never given a chance to go before God and make the speech he wanted to make. But the fact is, Job had no speech (argument) to make. God had not treated him unfairly. To claim so was pure ignorance. Job did not know as much as he thought he did.

No. 3. Job's life had not brought God into his debt. God did not owe him health and prosperity as a result of his good life. It was all a gift from God. I have been tempted to describe the subject of the book as *Justification by Faith*, and to see it as being a kind of *Romans in the Old Testament*, just as many have found reason to call Isaiah *The Romans of the Old Testament*. Paul's allusion to Job 41.10–11 in Romans 11.33–36 certainly teaches us that the two books have much in common. But I guess I decided at last it was an oversimplication. So we will have to be content with finding a good sermon on *Justification by Faith* in Job, while recognizing that the book as a whole may not be quite that limited.

No. 4. Job's wealth was certainly restored. But I suspect he looked on his restored fortune with different eyes, seeing it as a gift of grace as opposed to a reward merited by good conduct, and therefore with a heart filled with gratitude, humility, and a greater sense of his debt to his creator.

No. 5. Job's suffering had a divine purpose quite independent of Satan's purpose. Trial brought out some weaknesses and defects in Job that may have remained quite hidden without it, and so had produced healing at last. Job was a better man at the end than at the beginning of the book.

No. 6. Always looking for symmetry and order in a piece of literature, whether Biblical or otherwise, I guess I would tend to see the main point as an answer to Satan's taunts. Thus the epilogue corresponds to the prologue. Satan denied the existence of genuine piety, even in the man God declares to be the best on earth. He charged that Job was living the pious life only for the rewards, and, in effect, was only serving himself—not God. His piety was not genuine; it was a fake. The charge was an accusation against Job, of course, but even more a slander against God. No one will serve you, he charges, unless you pay him to do it; and what glory is that to you? The patience of Job exposed Satan for what he is, a liar and a slanderer. By clinging to God through it all (howbeit not without sin) Job vindicated and thus gave glory to God. Suffering may provide us with our greatest opportunity to serve and thus to give glory to God.

Also by L. A. Mott

Thinking Through Jeremiah

When Jesus came, some of his contemporaries thought that he was Jeremiah reincarnated. Yet many Bible students today know less about him than about a host of other Old Testament heroes. One who turns to commentaries for help will find that many of them are filled with complex discussions of strange Hebrew words and consideration of technical, critical questions with which most of us are totally unconcerned. A serious Bible student wishing to know Jeremiah and to understand his character, his preaching and his times will be grateful for L. A. Mott's *Thinking Through Jeremiah*. Foreword by Sewell Hall. 214 pages. $12.99 (PB)

Beneath the Cross: Essays and Relfections on the Lord's Supper
Jady S. Copeland and Nathan Ward (editors)

The Bible has much to say about the Lord's Supper. Almost every component of this memorial is rich with meaning—meaning supplied by Old Testament foreshadowing and New Testament teaching. The Lord's death itself is meaningful and significant in ways we rarely point out. In sixty-nine essays by forty different authors, Beneath the Cross explores the depths of symbolism and meaning to be found in the last hours of the Lord's life and offers a helpful look at the memorial feast that commemorates it. 329 pages. $14.99 (PB); $23.99 (HB).

Invitation to a Spiritual Revolution
Paul Earnhart

Few preachers have studied the Sermon on the Mount as intensively or spoken on its contents so frequently and effectively as the author of this work. His excellent and very readable written analysis appeared first as a series of articles in Christianity Magazine. By popular demand it is here offered in one volume so that it can be more easily preserved, circulated, read, reread and made available to those who would not otherwise have access to it. Foreword by Sewell Hall. 173 pages. $10.99 (PB)

Boot Camp
Jason Hardin

According to best-selling author Stephen Arterburn, "This is a great book to help us men live opposite of this world's model of a man." Boot Camp: Equipping Men with Integrity for Spiritual Warfare is the first volume in the new IMAGE series of books for men by Jason Hardin. It serves as a Basic Training manual in the spiritual war for honor, integrity and a God-glorifying life. 237 pages. $13.99 (PB); $24.99 (HB).

The Slave of Christ
Seth Parr

Immerse yourself in a place where sacrifice is reasonable, love and action are sensible, victory is guaranteed, and evangelism explodes. While the sacrifice of Jesus opens the door for us to Heaven, we must work to be conformed into His very image. In The Slave of Christ, uncover what biblical service means and how it can change your life. Energize your spiritual walk and awaken the servant within. 96 pags. $8.99 (PB)

HERITAGE
OF FAITH LIBRARY

The **DeWard Publishing Company Heritage of Faith Library** is a growing collection of classic Christian reprints. DeWard has already published or has plans to publish the following authors:

- A. B. Bruce
- Atticus G. Haygood
- H.C. Leupold
- J. W. McGarvey
- William Paley
- Albertus Pieters

Future authors and titles added to this series will be announced on our website.

www.dewardpublishing.com

DEWARD
PUBLISHING COMPANY

CPSIA information can be obtained at www.ICGtesting.com
Printed in the USA
LVOW091601261111

256557LV00002B/200/P